Miss Patti's Cook Book

McClanahan
Publishing House

Internation Standard Book Number 0 913383 51 5
Library of Congress Catalog Card Number 97 071893

Cover design and book layout by James Asher Graphics.
Front cover photograph by Bob McLean.
Back cover water color art by LaRue.
Project liaisons: Kay Alexander and Anita Locke

Manufactured in the United States of America.

McClanahan Publishing House, Inc.
P. O. Box 100
Kuttawa, KY 42055
(502) 388 9388
1 800 544 6959

Table of Contents

      *I*n this book, readers will dis-
cover "Miss Patti" , the woman behind Patti's and the recipes
and reflections she shares. Tidbits of the restaurant history,
memories, accolades and awards mix with the wonderful
recipes of Miss Patti, including those recipes she made as a
child right up to present creations like the ever popular boo
boo pie, are all here to enjoy. Welcome to her family!

Left to right, Michael T, Bill, Ronnie, me, Chip and Craig, 1957.

To all our friends, let me explain why I'm doing this book now. In 1995 I developed Lou Gehrig's disease, and in 1996 Bill developed a chronic lung disease. We don't have a long time left so we decided we needed to get on the stick and create the cookbook which everyone has asked us to do for years. The other reason for this book is to tell the story of my family for my grand and great grandchildren, and for their children. I also want the people who read my family's history to understand that yes, we have our oddities, but Bill and I, have always loved our children as we have loved each other these past 53 years. The love I've raised my family in has been an unconditional and non-judgmental love, as you will experience with the following words, and I'm very proud of my family. This is a story of my family and our success in bringing to our customers a special place, where friends bring friends, to relax, enjoy and experience the love an American family can really have for each other. A family who still has three generations working together.

This book is dedicated to my four wonderful children and their extended families, my grandchildren and great grandchildren, to all the employees and customers, past and present, who have helped us build this "oh, so wonderful a place".

Thank you all for your love and support. I hope you will treasure the memories of my family like I do all of your families.

Patti Tullar

J was born Patricia Ann Perry and I grew up in Chicago where my father was an architect who designed all the Warner Brothers theatres in the 1930s in and around Chicago. When I was a teenager, we moved to Tucson because Dad's health was poor and so was my mother's. In Tucson, he was the supervising architect at Fort Huahuca, Arizona for the Dell Webb Company.

When the family moved out west, I assumed the role

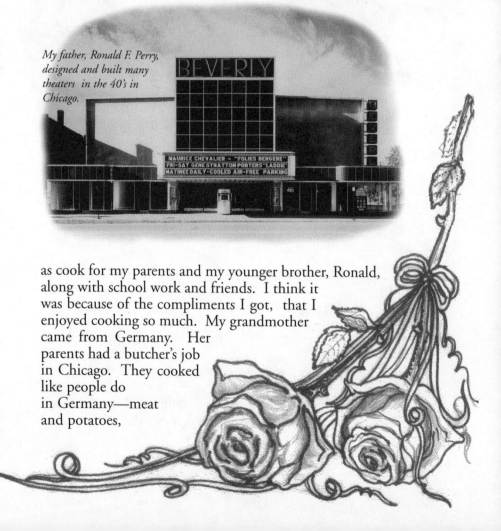

My father, Ronald F. Perry, designed and built many theaters in the 40's in Chicago.

as cook for my parents and my younger brother, Ronald, along with school work and friends. I think it was because of the compliments I got, that I enjoyed cooking so much. My grandmother came from Germany. Her parents had a butcher's job in Chicago. They cooked like people do in Germany—meat and potatoes,

vegetables, every night.
Desserts, too. I grew up cooking
that way."

*My brother Ronald
and me with goat pulling cart.*

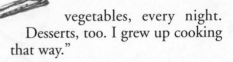

How Patti Got Started Cooking

When I was a young girl in Tucson, my mother became
very ill. She had a hole in her heart, and in
those days doctors didn't have all the miracu-
lous surgical techniques they have now. My
mother would lie in bed and
direct my activities in the
kitchen, and in time I
began to develop real
culinary skills. I remem-
ber the best present I

My baby brother who owns a large cattle ranch in Arizona. I really love him and I'm sure he loves me too.

ever got was when I received a Sunbeam Mix Master at the age of 14. Even my mother roused herself out of her sickbed to see it. It revolutionized my work in the kitchen —I remember having to smash boiled potatoes with a mallet to make mashed potatoes before I got the Mix Master, and it was so much easier and more fun to put the potatoes in and whip them into smoothness.

My father liked desserts most of all, so I concentrated on baking and became adept at making pies and cakes. He was allergic to egg whites, and every morning he ate two fried egg yolks for breakfast. I had jars and jars

of egg whites in the house as a result, and I used them up by making angel food cakes for all my friends and family. My mother and father praised my cooking to the skies, and I was hooked for life on what would eventually become my stock-in-trade. Here is my recipe for angel food cake.

Angel Food Cake

1 cup sifted cake flour
3/4 cup sugar
1-1/2 cups egg whites (12) at room temperature
1-1/2 teaspoons cream of tartar
1/4 teaspoon salt
1-1/2 teaspoons vanilla
3/4 cup sugar

Sift flour with 3/4 cup sugar 2 times; set aside. Beat egg whites with cream of tartar, salt and vanilla until stiff enough to form soft peaks but still moist and glossy. Add remaining 3/4 cup sugar, 2 tablespoons at a time; continue to beat until egg whites hold stiff peaks. Sift about 1/4 of flour mixture over whites; fold in. Repeat folding in remaining flour by fourths. Pour into ungreased 10 inch tube pan and bake at 375° for 35 to 40 minutes or until done. Invert cake in pan; cool.

My brother and I went to high school in Tombstone. It was fun to go to a little school when you were used to big ones back in Chicago. We always had animals growing up and I rode horses, even to school.

But my best ride ever was to the hospital when I met a young man named Bill Tullar, while I was visiting a family friend next to him in the V.A. hospital in Tucson.

The friend's parents were my parents' friends, from Chicago, and since Bob was a long way from home, they asked me if I would visit their eighteen year-old, paraplegic son (who, by the way, was the first paraplegic to return from WWII) and take along some of my girlfriends. We often visited and entertained the service men who were wounded. It didn't take long for me to strike up conversation with young Bill Tullar and, the rest is history.

Bill, 1939

When Ronnie was only 3 months old, I moved back in with my mom and dad when Bill returned to the hospital for a two-year stay with tuberculosis.

All the children were born in

Our engagement day.

Tucson. Bill took a job with an insurance company and we moved to California and later in the '50s we moved to Hawaii for six and one half years, returning to California in 1963.

During our life in Hawaii, the children didn't wear shoes until jr high school. The cli-

Patti & Bill's Wedding, May 18, 1945

mate was warm but even when it was cooler, children wore sweaters but no shoes. People only wore shorts, mumus, bathing suits—it truly was a great life.

Our family ate lots of rice and pineapples. Living on the island, everyone ate great amounts of fruit, especially mangos and papayas. We had mango trees on our property and Chip would crawl up the

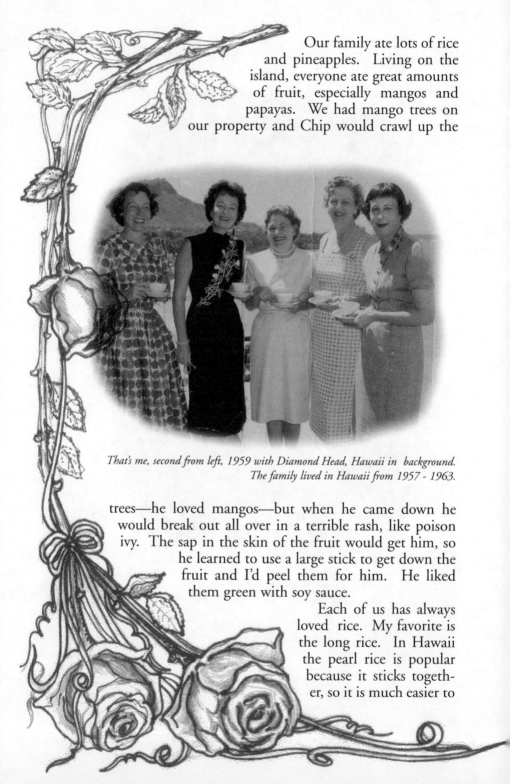

That's me, second from left, 1959 with Diamond Head, Hawaii in background.
The family lived in Hawaii from 1957 - 1963.

trees—he loved mangos—but when he came down he would break out all over in a terrible rash, like poison ivy. The sap in the skin of the fruit would get him, so he learned to use a large stick to get down the fruit and I'd peel them for him. He liked them green with soy sauce.

Each of us has always loved rice. My favorite is the long rice. In Hawaii the pearl rice is popular because it sticks together, so it is much easier to

eat with chop sticks.
There are all different kinds of
rice and each cooks up differently.
      I never knew how to cook
rice, although I tried a number of
times. No matter what I did it would turn
into a starchy mess that stuck together and
would have to be thrown away. While living in Hawaii in
the 1950s, I had a GE electric stove that was supposed to
automatically regulate the oven heat, and it didn't work cor-
rectly. The GE repairman sent to fix the oven was Japanese,
and he spent more time at my house than anyone else's
house on the island. He was there so much that we became
friends, and he taught me how to make perfect, never-
fail rice.

Patti's Perfect Rice

*Measure one part raw rice for every two parts of cooked
rice desired (e.g. 1 cup raw rice will make two cups cooked rice).
Wash the raw rice and spread it evenly in a cooking pot. Place
the tip of your index finger on the top of the rice and add
enough water so that the first knuckle is completely covered
with water (approximately two cups water to one cup rice, but
the first knuckle measurement is more accurate and more fun).
Add a lump of butter and bring it to a boil. Stir well, put the
lid on the pot, turn the heat down as low as it will go, and leave
the pot undisturbed for 20 minutes. The rice will be perfect
every time.*

      Aftermath to the stove story: When
the Tullar family left the Islands to return to
the states we sold the stove to one of our
friends. The friends invited
us over for a good-bye
party, and to my chagrin,
the stove chose that day
of all days to burn up
completely.   Fire

engines had to be summoned to put out the flames. That stove was a lemon from start to finish, but because of it I now know the secret of perfect rice.

Me in 1961. We just moved from Hawaii, Bill was promoted to Area Director for John Hancock Life Insurance Company. I really enjoyed dressing up and entertaining.

I remember seeing the little straw houses or huts in Hawaii, they were fishing houses on stilts, where people sit and fish. One day I saw a lady with her fishing pole and string in the water and much to my amazement the woman had her little son on the other end of the line—his bathing suit hooked to her line so he could swim but so "mama" could reel him back to safety! That was one of the funniest sights I remember. Most kids knew how to swim but I guess this little fellow did not. My children were like ducks, always in the water swimming.

We lived in a suburb of Waikiki and there we rented an old beach house and lived on the water. All of our friends had little sailboats and they would come over on weekends and we'd go sailing. Michael was only two so he had to have a bubble on his back so he wouldn't drown.

People rented old beach houses and they were cheap. We really loved it and had a wonderful time. We didn't have to heat or cool anything. One time I had friends over to play bridge and the weather turned cold unexpectedly. So we all bundled up and sat around the card table positioned right in front of the opened oven door to keep warm! We didn't have warm clothing so we just had to make do.

Liquid Smoke Adds Just Right Flavor To Barbecued Ribs, Mrs. Tullar Says

IN LIEU OF PARSLEY, Mrs. William G. Tullar garnishes a platter of barbecued ribs with sprigs of mint from her yard. This decoration looks just as pretty, and smells good, too. As for the ribs, which also appear most enticing, Mrs. Tullar says they are easy to fix and tells us just how it's done in our cooking corner this week. The meat dish is a family favorite at the Tullar home, 4874 East Scarlett. (Levitz Photo)

That's me in a newspaper article with ribs, 1954.

Big breakfasts were a must in the Tullar household in the early days. We always had to have a big breakfast, because the kids were on swim teams and very active. Well, I couldn't cook for four kids and get them out the door on time, especially because they liked waffles, pancakes, eggs and egg sandwiches. So my solution to this was to have two waffle irons going at the same time to help with the rush. My tip for handling this hustle and bustle more smoothly—pick up an extra waffle iron at a yard sale one weekend!

For grown-up breakfasts, try two of my favorite recipes, Derby Day Grits and Southern Fried Apples. These are sure to please hungry guests and family.

First place in hat decorating contest on USS Matisonia on our way from Hawaii to Los Angeles. Chip was 11 years old, 6'2", 125 pounds. I knew he had a talent to decorate.

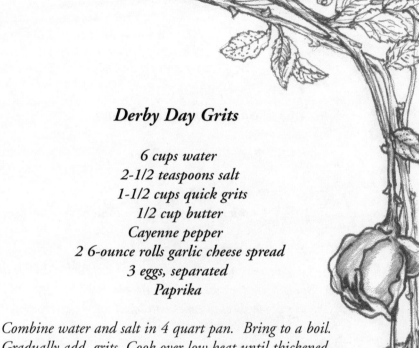

Derby Day Grits

6 cups water
2-1/2 teaspoons salt
1-1/2 cups quick grits
1/2 cup butter
Cayenne pepper
2 6-ounce rolls garlic cheese spread
3 eggs, separated
Paprika

Combine water and salt in 4 quart pan. Bring to a boil.
Gradually add grits. Cook over low heat until thickened.
Remove from heat. Mix in butter, cayenne and cheese; stir
until cheese melts. Stir in yolks. Beat whites until stiff; fold
in. Pour in greased casserole dish. Bake at 350° for 45 minutes to 1 hour or until they begin to set.

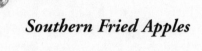

Southern Fried Apples

6 medium size cooking apples
1/3 cup butter
2/3 cup sugar
1 tablespoon ground cinnamon
Dash salt

Core but do not peel apples. Slice 1/2 inch thick to
make perfect rings.   Heat butter in heavy skillet. Fit
in the apple slices to cover bottom of skillet without
breaking the slices. Mix sugar with cinnamon and salt
and cover apples with one-half the mixture. Cook slowly for
5 minutes; turn slices with a pancake turner to avoid breaking. Cover with remaining sugar mixture and cook over low
heat until apples are almost transparent. If too well done they
will break easily. Serve hot. Yield: 6 servings

I'd always ask on Saturday what the kids wanted for lunch, grilled peanut butter and jelly or grilled cheese sandwich because I only had one frying pan in those days. At the restaurant, we cook it on the grill with butter on the homemade bread and it's toasty and the warm peanut butter is soft and yummy. My kids like the jelly sandwiches the best. Today, Grilled Peanut Butter and Bananas are crowd pleasers.

Grilled Peanut Butter & Jelly Sandwich

Cook just like a grilled cheese sandwich. They are wonderful cut up as appetizers too!

Chip worked his way through high school paying his own way to Hawaii for summer of 1967. Michael, Craig and I welcome him home.

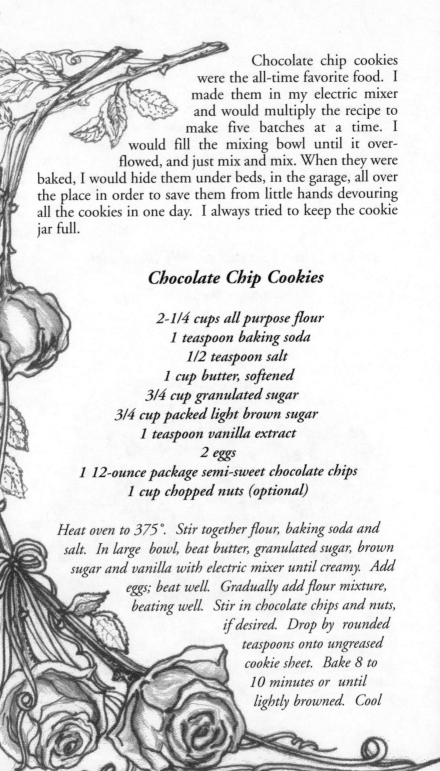

Chocolate chip cookies were the all-time favorite food. I made them in my electric mixer and would multiply the recipe to make five batches at a time. I would fill the mixing bowl until it over-flowed, and just mix and mix. When they were baked, I would hide them under beds, in the garage, all over the place in order to save them from little hands devouring all the cookies in one day. I always tried to keep the cookie jar full.

Chocolate Chip Cookies

2-1/4 cups all purpose flour
1 teaspoon baking soda
1/2 teaspoon salt
1 cup butter, softened
3/4 cup granulated sugar
3/4 cup packed light brown sugar
1 teaspoon vanilla extract
2 eggs
1 12-ounce package semi-sweet chocolate chips
1 cup chopped nuts (optional)

Heat oven to 375°. Stir together flour, baking soda and salt. In large bowl, beat butter, granulated sugar, brown sugar and vanilla with electric mixer until creamy. Add eggs; beat well. Gradually add flour mixture, beating well. Stir in chocolate chips and nuts, if desired. Drop by rounded teaspoons onto ungreased cookie sheet. Bake 8 to 10 minutes or until lightly browned. Cool

*slightly; remove from cookie
sheet to wire rack.*

*Pan recipe: Prepare batter as
above. Spread in greased 15-1/2x10-1/2x1
inch jelly roll pan. Bake at 375° 20 minutes
or until lightly browned.   Cool completely in pan on wire
rack; cut into bars.*

About Our Blue Beetle Car

While we lived in Hawaii, when the kids
were little—in the 50's, I would drive the kids to the
beach to go surfing. I'd sit on that beach all day and
get "redder than a turnip." Why, I looked like a baked
tomato, but I'd watch them all day and enjoy it.

We had a DeSoto sedan, about a 1949 model. It was
a big old car, no power steering, nothing fancy. And on top
of that, the odometer was not right—and that's how I got
my first speeding ticket. Michael T. wasn't in school then
and I'd take him to Waikiki to swim. I would always go
what I believed to be the limit, but one day I got stopped.
Afterward, Michael said, 'Mom, the reason you got a ticket
was because the speedometer doesn't work!' Well, that was
the only ticket I ever got but I sure watched my sons get
tickets. They go much too fast. I could always tell when
they'd been pulled over because I would see the ticket
on the dashboard of the car when I got in and
would know they had been speeding.

When the kids were little, they were
in charge of dishes. When
we had company I'd pay
them 50 cents an hour
extra to do the dishes.
They did yard work

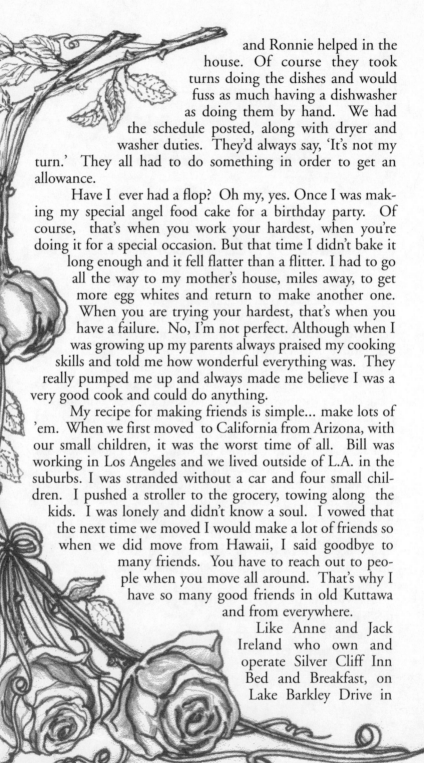

and Ronnie helped in the house. Of course they took turns doing the dishes and would fuss as much having a dishwasher as doing them by hand. We had the schedule posted, along with dryer and washer duties. They'd always say, 'It's not my turn.' They all had to do something in order to get an allowance.

Have I ever had a flop? Oh my, yes. Once I was making my special angel food cake for a birthday party. Of course, that's when you work your hardest, when you're doing it for a special occasion. But that time I didn't bake it long enough and it fell flatter than a flitter. I had to go all the way to my mother's house, miles away, to get more egg whites and return to make another one. When you are trying your hardest, that's when you have a failure. No, I'm not perfect. Although when I was growing up my parents always praised my cooking skills and told me how wonderful everything was. They really pumped me up and always made me believe I was a very good cook and could do anything.

My recipe for making friends is simple... make lots of 'em. When we first moved to California from Arizona, with our small children, it was the worst time of all. Bill was working in Los Angeles and we lived outside of L.A. in the suburbs. I was stranded without a car and four small children. I pushed a stroller to the grocery, towing along the kids. I was lonely and didn't know a soul. I vowed that the next time we moved I would make a lot of friends so when we did move from Hawaii, I said goodbye to many friends. You have to reach out to people when you move all around. That's why I have so many good friends in old Kuttawa and from everywhere.

Like Anne and Jack Ireland who own and operate Silver Cliff Inn Bed and Breakfast, on Lake Barkley Drive in old Kuttawa, only a few minutes away from Grand Rivers.

Bill and I often share guests with them. Following are a couple of Anne's special breakfast recipes which are served in the atmosphere of a lazy-morning, outdoor patio breakfast overlooking Lake Barkley or, in winter, a cozy setting in front of a roaring fire.

Annie's Mayonnaise Biscuits

1 cup self-rising flour
1 cup milk (sweet or buttermilk)
1 tablespoon mayonnaise

Mix flour, milk and mayonnaise. Spoon into muffin pan and bake at 425 degrees for 10-15 minutes. Recipe can be doubled. Makes 6 biscuits.

Ann Ireland, Silver Cliff Inn

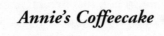

Annie's Coffeecake

2 tablespoons light brown sugar
1 teaspoon ground cinnamon
1 box butter yellow cake mix
1/2 cup sugar
1 8-ounce carton sour cream
1/4 teaspoon salt
3/4 cup vegetable oil
4 eggs
2 teaspoons vanilla
1/2 cup chopped pecans

Mix together brown sugar and cinnamon. Set aside. Mix cake mix, sugar, sour cream, salt, oil, eggs, vanilla and pecans. Pour half of batter in greased Bundt or tube pan. Sprinkle brown sugar and cinnamon mixture over batter. Add rest of batter. Bake 45 minutes to 1 hour at 350°.

Anne Ireland, Silver Cliff Inn

My children are
fond of cooking. Michael, who
was a high school senior while we
lived in Germany, was fascinated
with all the table-side preparations
in restaurants. The German waiters knew
how to put on a show when they made salads,
sauces and desserts right beside your table. Michael loved
to watch and then when he got home he experimented.
Years later when Patti's on the Pier opened, it was Michael
who implemented such spectacular Sunday brunch buffet
foods as freshly prepared omelets and waffles, Baked Alaska
and Flaming Cherries Jubilee. Here's a sample.

Cherries Jubilee

1 16-ounce can pitted, dark sweet cherries
1/4 cup sugar
2 tablespoons cornstarch
1/4 cup brandy, kirsch or cherry brandy
Vanilla ice cream

Drain cherries; reserve syrup adding water to make 1 cup. In
saucepan, blend sugar and cornstarch; gradually add cherry
syrup. Cook and stir over medium heat until mixture thick-
ens and bubbles. Remove from heat; stir in cherries. Turn
into heat-proof bowl. Heat brandy. Ignite the brandy
and pour or ladle over cherry mixture. Blend into sauce
and serve immediately over ice cream. Makes
2 cups.

During our stay in Germany, I learned to cook German food. I prepared lots of noodle dishes and, of course, many kinds of sausages, so typical of the German style.

I belonged to the German-American Club, and once a month the American women cooked for the German women and vice versa. We met interesting women and certainly increased our cooking skills. Again I cooked with clay, often baking roasts and other meats in the oven, using this slow-cooking technique.

From Germany we moved to Florida and finally to Kentucky, where I practiced the only thing I knew how to do and that was to cook.

Ronnie's Favorite Pot Roast

Any size pot roast
1 bottle ketchup
1 bottle beer

Place pot roast in crock pot and pour ketchup and beer over roast. Cook all day lone on low. Serve over cooked noodles. Beer tenderizes the meat and ketchup gives the roast flavor.

Chip with winning bill board and smile. Humboldt State College, Arcadia, California, 1967.

Chip with catch of the day, 1968.

Grandma Tullar, Bill, me, Ronnie, Mike, 1968.

Our four children, 1996. Left to right, bottom row, Bill, me, Craig, top row, Chip, Ronnie, Michael.

Ronnie's high school graduation.
Left to right, me, Grandma
Tullar and Ronnie.

Left to right, Craig, Mike, Chip,
Bill at Trinidad Bay near
Arcadia, California at Chip's
first year in college.

Mike, Craig, Chip, 1996

*H*amburger Patti's Ice Cream Parlor was opened by Bill, Patti, Chip and Michael Lee in 1977. True to its name, the restaurant specialized in terrific hamburgers and mouth-watering homemade ice cream.

Grand Rivers, Kentucky seemed an unlikely place for the Tullars to settle, but Bill had fallen in love with this tiny

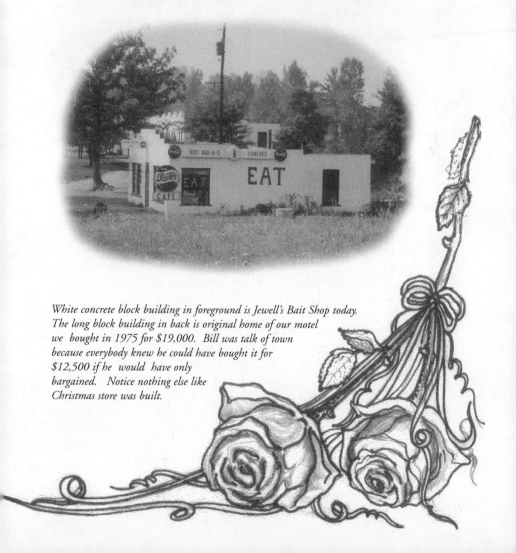

White concrete block building in foreground is Jewell's Bait Shop today. The long block building in back is original home of our motel we bought in 1975 for $19,000. Bill was talk of town because everybody knew he could have bought it for $12,500 if he would have only bargained. Notice nothing else like Christmas store was built.

hamlet while stationed in western Kentucky as an investigator for the United States government's disaster relief program, FEMA. After visiting the area, Patti discovered she shared Bill's vision for the slower paced life in the resort community. Soon afterward, we purchased Newcomb's Modern Cabins, a small motel, costing only $19,000. "Where we came from

Original Hamburger Patti's Ice Cream. Opening picture, May, 1977. See our outdoor dining area. One table - if you stand at hostess station today you'll see this front porch has been engulfed by additions.

in California you couldn't even buy a garage for $19,000. So we thought it was a great deal and I didn't even bargain for it. In this deal we bought the whole motel with 5 kitchens and 5 baths plus two cottages. Some folks said I paid too much but Patti and I felt this was an untapped area," Mr. Bill recalls.

1977 - our opening menu.

SANDWICHES

WE OFFER YOUR CHOICES OF WHEAT, RYE, WHITE, OR SESAME SEED BUN.
OUR SANDWICHES SERVED WITH PICKLES & POTATO CHIPS.

PATTI'S — 1/4 lb. 100% ground chuck charbroiled hamburger served on a SESAME SEED BUN. 1.25
With Cheese $1.35

BILL'S JR. BURGER — 3 oz. charbroiled 100% ground chuck.................. .95
With Cheese 1.05

GRAND MA'S — charbroiled hamburger simmered in our savory bar-b-que sauce... 1.65

MICHELLE'S — open faced broiled Swiss Cheese, Onion, Tomato,
and Garlic Butter with HAM 1.85

STEVE'S — 1/4 lb charbroiled ground beef with melted cheese, grilled onions,
and served on Grilled Rye Toast. 1.55

SLICED HAM — with Mustard, Lettuce, and Sliced Tomatoes 1.75
Swiss or American Cheese 1.85

SLICED TURKEY — with Lettuce, and Mayonnaise. 1.75
Swiss or American Cheese 1.85

SLICED ROAST BEEF — with Lettuce, Tomato, and Mayonnaise............. 1.85
Swiss or American Cheese 1.95

GRILLED CHEESE .... .70
PEANUT BUTTER & JELLY .... .70
MIKE'S CORN DOG .... (Piping Hot) .55
CHIP'S Coney Island Dogs with Delicious Sauce .... (Foot Long) 1.50
TERRY'S Regular Foot Long Hot Dog (Your Choice Of Condiments) 1.00
FRENCH FRIES.. .60
ONION RINGS... .75

OUR CONDIMENTS

SWISS CHEESE .... AMERICAN CHEESE
TOMATOES .... LETTUCE
PICKLES .... RELISH
MUSTARD .... MAYONNAISE
CATSUP .... ONIONS

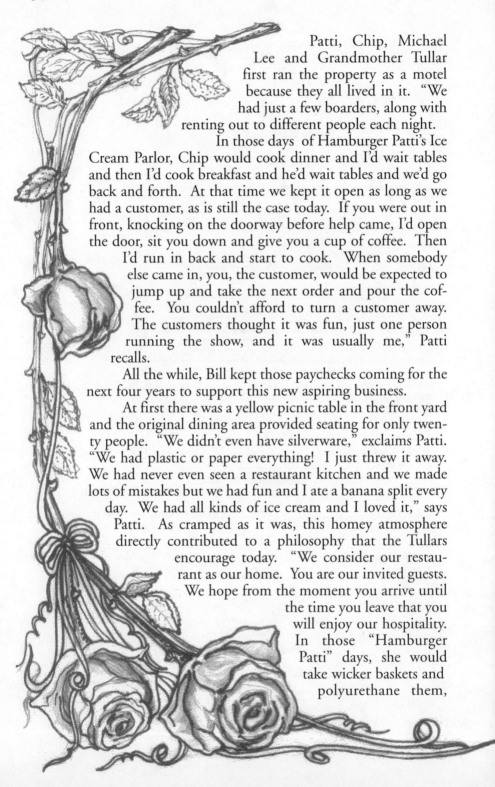

Patti, Chip, Michael Lee and Grandmother Tullar first ran the property as a motel because they all lived in it. "We had just a few boarders, along with renting out to different people each night.

In those days of Hamburger Patti's Ice Cream Parlor, Chip would cook dinner and I'd wait tables and then I'd cook breakfast and he'd wait tables and we'd go back and forth. At that time we kept it open as long as we had a customer, as is still the case today. If you were out in front, knocking on the doorway before help came, I'd open the door, sit you down and give you a cup of coffee. Then I'd run in back and start to cook. When somebody else came in, you, the customer, would be expected to jump up and take the next order and pour the coffee. You couldn't afford to turn a customer away. The customers thought it was fun, just one person running the show, and it was usually me," Patti recalls.

All the while, Bill kept those paychecks coming for the next four years to support this new aspiring business.

At first there was a yellow picnic table in the front yard and the original dining area provided seating for only twenty people. "We didn't even have silverware," exclaims Patti. "We had plastic or paper everything! I just threw it away. We had never even seen a restaurant kitchen and we made lots of mistakes but we had fun and I ate a banana split every day. We had all kinds of ice cream and I loved it," says Patti. As cramped as it was, this homey atmosphere directly contributed to a philosophy that the Tullars encourage today. "We consider our restaurant as our home. You are our invited guests. We hope from the moment you arrive until the time you leave that you will enjoy our hospitality. In those "Hamburger Patti" days, she would take wicker baskets and polyurethane them, put a liner in for potato chips, pickles and the burger and didn't have to wash the baskets all the time. She would practice her recipes in the basement, when they moved into the "big" house and there she concocted jam cakes, bran muffins and all kinds of treats because the stove in the kitchen did not work. She still has the metal hamburger press her friend Mabel Nash, at the Iron Kettle, gave her.

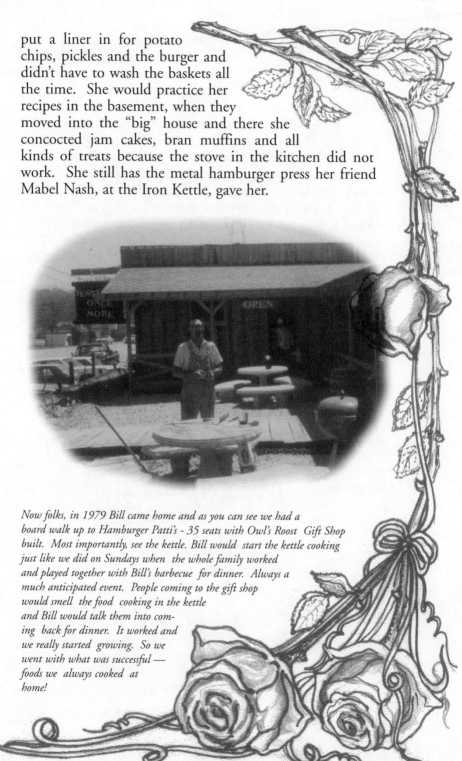

Now folks, in 1979 Bill came home and as you can see we had a board walk up to Hamburger Patti's - 35 seats with Owl's Roost Gift Shop built. Most importantly, see the kettle. Bill would start the kettle cooking just like we did on Sundays when the whole family worked and played together with Bill's barbecue for dinner. Always a much anticipated event. People coming to the gift shop would smell the food cooking in the kettle and Bill would talk them into com- ing back for dinner. It worked and we really started growing. So we went with what was successful — foods we always cooked at home!

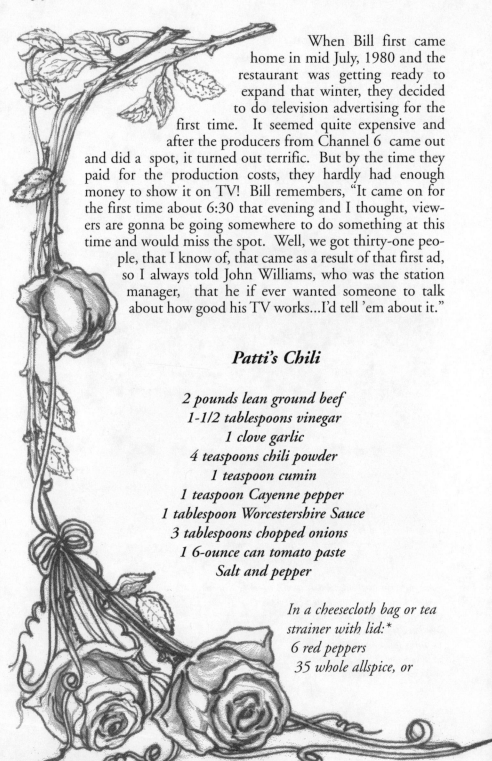

When Bill first came home in mid July, 1980 and the restaurant was getting ready to expand that winter, they decided to do television advertising for the first time. It seemed quite expensive and after the producers from Channel 6 came out and did a spot, it turned out terrific. But by the time they paid for the production costs, they hardly had enough money to show it on TV! Bill remembers, "It came on for the first time about 6:30 that evening and I thought, viewers are gonna be going somewhere to do something at this time and would miss the spot. Well, we got thirty-one people, that I know of, that came as a result of that first ad, so I always told John Williams, who was the station manager, that he if ever wanted someone to talk about how good his TV works...I'd tell 'em about it."

Patti's Chili

2 pounds lean ground beef
1-1/2 tablespoons vinegar
1 clove garlic
4 teaspoons chili powder
1 teaspoon cumin
1 teaspoon Cayenne pepper
1 tablespoon Worcestershire Sauce
3 tablespoons chopped onions
1 6-ounce can tomato paste
Salt and pepper

In a cheesecloth bag or tea strainer with lid:*
6 red peppers
35 whole allspice, or

1/4 teaspoon ground
   allspice
5 or 6 bay leaves

Mix all ingredients in a large saucepan.
Simmer slowly for three hours.

* May use 1/2 teaspoon red pepper and 1/2 teaspoon allspice
in place of these spices. If not hot enough, add more.

   Bill soon knew that they needed to merchandise
Patti's and get out the word, but how? They had the
kids who were working like heck but someone needed to get out among people and tell them about the
restaurant. So Bill became somewhat of an "ambas-

Patti's 1979 - note Trophy Room
Dining Room today used to be
Owl's Roost Gift Shop - our first
retail venture, 1979.

sador at large" and took vases of his beautiful roses, which he so lovingly grew and groomed, to the hospitals and to all the patients.

He would also put them at the cash registers of nearby hotels and motels such as the Holiday Inn, Kentucky Dam Village, and the Bel Air Motel—plus at the golf course, the Land Between the Lakes Visitor's Center and other tourist places. "I gave a rose to

Left to right, first row, Bill's dad Hilton Tullar, Keith, Kimberly, Bill's mother Delsa Tullar. Second row, Michael, Craig, our cousin Corey Tullar, Ronnie and Bill. Notice the overalls — always on Bill. Part of the Patti's picture.

these business people and gave everybody 2 free dinners at Patti's because I figured nobody would recommend people coming to Patti's if they

hadn't been there them-
selves. It worked. People came
and they loved it!" Each and

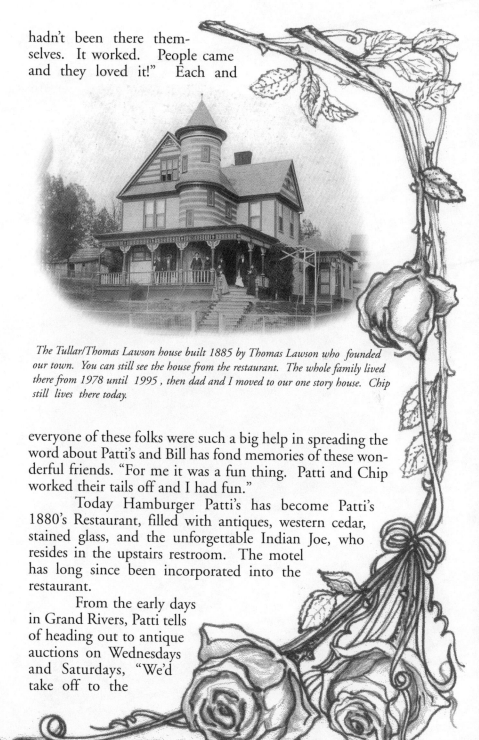

*The Tullar/Thomas Lawson house built 1885 by Thomas Lawson who founded
our town. You can still see the house from the restaurant. The whole family lived
there from 1978 until 1995, then dad and I moved to our one story house. Chip
still lives there today.*

everyone of these folks were such a big help in spreading the
word about Patti's and Bill has fond memories of these wonderful friends. "For me it was a fun thing. Patti and Chip
worked their tails off and I had fun."

Today Hamburger Patti's has become Patti's
1880's Restaurant, filled with antiques, western cedar,
stained glass, and the unforgettable Indian Joe, who
resides in the upstairs restroom. The motel
has long since been incorporated into the
restaurant.

From the early days
in Grand Rivers, Patti tells
of heading out to antique
auctions on Wednesdays
and Saturdays, "We'd
take off to the

antique auctions and put
a note on the door saying 'if
you want a room, just move in
and I'll take your money when I
come home.'"

*Grandmother Delsa Mortenson
Tullar at age 17 - 1915.
Graduated Albion Nursing
College in 1919. You were very
beautiful
Delsa.*

To this day she has a unique collection of antiques. "It was just funny because we'd come home with a big truck piled high with this primitive stuff and people would look out of the windows of their houses and car windows at all this stuff as we made our way back to the restaurant. But at that time I didn't have any furniture and I liked to refinish furniture so it was a sensible thing to do. We'd get the rectangular tables we now use in the dining rooms for less than $100. The round ones were more difficult to get."

Chicken Enchiladas

1 package flour tortillas
1 4-ounce can green diced chilies
1 pint sour cream
2 10-1/2 ounce cans cream of chicken soup
1 pound shredded Monterey Jack cheese
3 whole chicken breasts, boiled and diced
1 4-ounce can sliced ripe olives

In 9x13 inch pan, place half of the flour tortillas and chicken. Mix chilies, sour cream, soup and olives. Pour half of mixture over chicken. Cover with half of the cheese. Repeat the layers. Bake in 325° oven until bubbly. Serve with salsa, kidney beans and chili.

The food service side of Patti's has evolved into the menu items offered today. Patti's 1880's boasts of 2-inch thick charbroiled pork chops, "mile-high" meringue pies, and "flower pot" bread served with whipped or strawberry butter.

Bill and Grandmother Tullar at 94. She worked up until last three weeks of her life in the gift shop! She even was on TV because she was 99% blind, in a wheelchair, and still worked every day and memorized every price of every item in our gift shop. She was truly a person to admire.

Grand Opening of Patti's of Glasgow, 1986 - closed in 1988. We learned we just have more fun working close to each other.

Patti's of Glasgow 1880 farm house on 3-1/2 acres of beautifully landscaped property - prettiest restaurant you ever did see.

These specialties are original to Patti's, although none of the Tullar family or staff has ever

Bill Tullar as a child - can you see where the puppet thing came from!

had a professional cooking lesson. Basically, the aim of Patti's is to try to cook wholesome American food that

encompasses a wide variety
of tastes.

Bill and Colonel, the really good spitting llama.

In years past, Patti Tullar was respon-
sible for recipe development and quality
control in the baking divi-
sion, as well as performing
the personal duties associ-
ated with being "Miss
Patti" of Patti's 1880's
Restaurant.

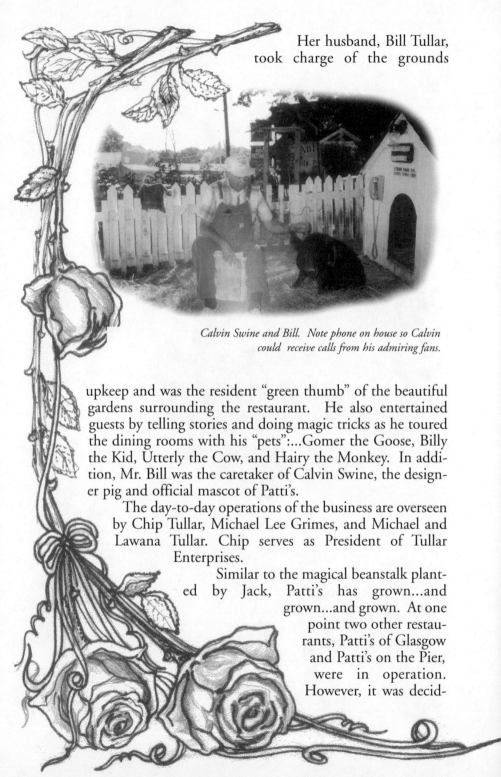

Her husband, Bill Tullar, took charge of the grounds

Calvin Swine and Bill. Note phone on house so Calvin could receive calls from his admiring fans.

upkeep and was the resident "green thumb" of the beautiful gardens surrounding the restaurant. He also entertained guests by telling stories and doing magic tricks as he toured the dining rooms with his "pets":...Gomer the Goose, Billy the Kid, Utterly the Cow, and Hairy the Monkey. In addition, Mr. Bill was the caretaker of Calvin Swine, the designer pig and official mascot of Patti's.

The day-to-day operations of the business are overseen by Chip Tullar, Michael Lee Grimes, and Michael and Lawana Tullar. Chip serves as President of Tullar Enterprises.

Similar to the magical beanstalk planted by Jack, Patti's has grown...and grown...and grown. At one point two other restaurants, Patti's of Glasgow and Patti's on the Pier, were in operation. However, it was decid-

ed that the ambiance and
quality of Patti's 1880 could best
be served by centralizing the business at the original location in
"downtown" Grand Rivers. With
that thought in mind, plans for the expansion of Patti's were drawn up in December of
1988. The first part of the expansion was completed in the
summer of 1990 with the addition of a larger kitchen, two
new dining rooms at Patti's, then the 1993 opening of an
adjoining venture—Mr. Bill's Bone Box, a fun-filled restaurant featuring ribs, chicken, and fish served with bountiful
portions of home-cooked vegetables. Named after Bill
Tullar, Mr. Bill's was Kentucky Lake's most delightful,
fun place to eat. In addition, the best musical enter-
tainment this side of Nashville was featured nightly.
Today this side of the restaurant serves the same fine
dishes as Patti's.

Patti's on the Pier 1984-1988

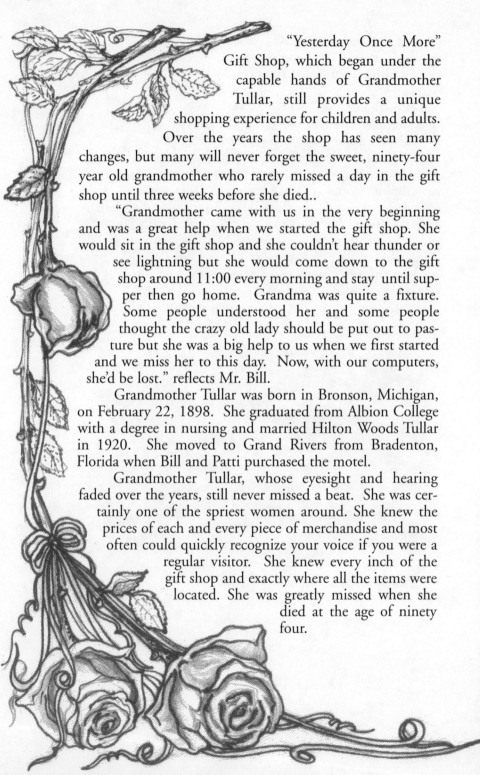

"Yesterday Once More" Gift Shop, which began under the capable hands of Grandmother Tullar, still provides a unique shopping experience for children and adults.

Over the years the shop has seen many changes, but many will never forget the sweet, ninety-four year old grandmother who rarely missed a day in the gift shop until three weeks before she died..

"Grandmother came with us in the very beginning and was a great help when we started the gift shop. She would sit in the gift shop and she couldn't hear thunder or see lightning but she would come down to the gift shop around 11:00 every morning and stay until supper then go home. Grandma was quite a fixture. Some people understood her and some people thought the crazy old lady should be put out to pasture but she was a big help to us when we first started and we miss her to this day. Now, with our computers, she'd be lost." reflects Mr. Bill.

Grandmother Tullar was born in Bronson, Michigan, on February 22, 1898. She graduated from Albion College with a degree in nursing and married Hilton Woods Tullar in 1920. She moved to Grand Rivers from Bradenton, Florida when Bill and Patti purchased the motel.

Grandmother Tullar, whose eyesight and hearing faded over the years, still never missed a beat. She was certainly one of the spriest women around. She knew the prices of each and every piece of merchandise and most often could quickly recognize your voice if you were a regular visitor. She knew every inch of the gift shop and exactly where all the items were located. She was greatly missed when she died at the age of ninety four.

Red Velvet Cake

1/2 cup butter
1-1/2 cups sugar
2 eggs
2 ounces red food coloring
2 heaping tablespoons cocoa
1 cup buttermilk
2-1/4 cups self-rising flour
1/2 teaspoon salt
1 teaspoon vanilla
1 teaspoon soda
1 tablespoon vinegar

In large bowl, cream together butter, sugar and eggs. Make a
paste out of the red food coloring and cocoa and add to egg
mixture. Add buttermilk, flour and salt and mix well. In
separate bowl, mix together vanilla, soda and vinegar. Fold
into mixture. Pour into 3 greased and floured 8" baking
pans. Bake at 325° for 25 to 30 minutes or until wooden
pick comes out clean.

This recipe is similar to one Patti made when
she was a girl. "But we didn't have self-rising flour," she exclaims!

Patti's is almost as famous for their decorations as they are for their fine food.

An estimated $20,000. is spent annually on the purchase and acquisition of new decorations. Often visitors stop in for the sole purpose of touring the restaurant and viewing the lovely decor. The talented lady in charge of interior decorations is Marian Bauguss with Barbara McAbee becoming lead decorator as of Christmas, 1996.

Decorations are changed several times during the year. Each new season is welcomed and extra attention is given to important events like New Year's, Valentine's Day, Easter, Memorial Day, the Fourth of July, Labor Day, Halloween, Thanksgiving and Christmas. Of course, there's a yearly presentation of handmade quilts to correspond with the National Quilt Show held in late April in nearby Paducah.

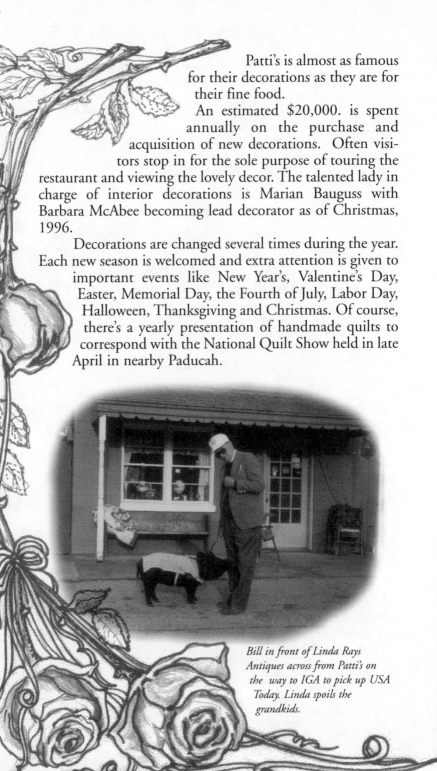

Bill in front of Linda Rays Antiques across from Patti's on the way to IGA to pick up USA Today. Linda spoils the grandkids.

The most renown
of pets at Patti's is Calvin Swine, a
miniature African pig, who lives in
the lap of luxury. He has his very
own house, his own wardrobe complete with bib overalls, and drinks lemonade
to his heart's content. Mr. Bill and Calvin used to take
leisurely walks around Grand Rivers late in the afternoon.
Calvin wears a leash...but that's only because he doesn't
want Mr. Bill to get lost!

A "don't miss" sight at Patti's is sure to be Indian Joe.
Guests will find him resting comfortably and very much at
home in the upstairs restroom.

Prior to moving to surely the nation's most
photographed restroom, Indian Joe spent his days at
a local antique shop. Chip visited the shop often
and tried unsuccessfully for years to purchase the
wooden Indian for the restaurant. The owner could
not bear to part with his trusted companion and
refused to sell the old boy. Chip resigned himself to

Bill and the famous spitting Yama Lama.

Patti's Jam Cake

2 cups sugar
1 cup butter
6 eggs, separated
1 cup buttermilk
2 teaspoons baking soda
1 teaspoon baking powder
4 cups flour
1 teaspoon cinnamon
1 teaspoon cocoa
1 teaspoon allspice
1 teaspoon vanilla
2 cups blackberry jam
1 cup raisins
2 cups black walnuts, chopped

Combine sugar and butter. Add egg yolks; beat until light
and fluffy. Stir baking soda into buttermilk until baking
soda is dissolved. Sift baking powder, flour, cinnamon,
cocoa, and allspice together. Add sifted dry ingredients to
egg yolk mixture alternately with buttermilk. Mix until
smooth; add jam, raisins and walnuts by hand.
Mix thoroughly. Pour into two 9" greased
and floured round pans and bake at 350° for
about 50 minutes. Check
at 45 minutes. Frost with
caramel icing or your
favorite frosting.

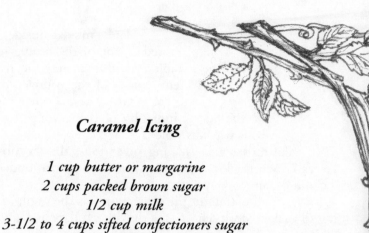

Caramel Icing

1 cup butter or margarine
2 cups packed brown sugar
1/2 cup milk
3-1/2 to 4 cups sifted confectioners sugar

Melt butter over medium heat. Stir in sugar and milk.
Bring to a boil. Remove from heat; cool until just
warm. With an electric mixer, beat in enough of the
confectioners sugar until spreading consistency is
reached.

Patti always makes this recipe during Christmas but wonders,
"why don't we make it more often? It's delicious."

the fact that Indian Joe would never become a part of the
Patti's family.

Later, the shop's proprietor became seriously ill
and was forced to close his business. At that time, he
decided that the only person who thought as much of
Indian Joe as he did was Chip Tullar. He
called Chip and told him that he could finally buy the Indian. Earl Lee, your
memory lives on.

Upon arrival at the
restaurant, Indian Joe was
positioned on the front
steps at Patti's. He was

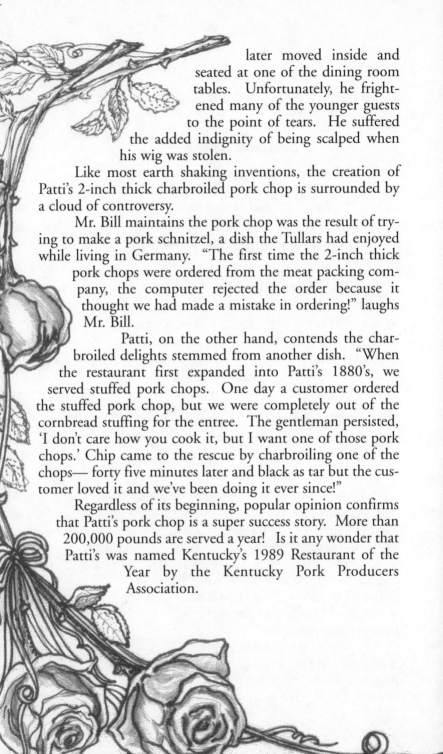

later moved inside and seated at one of the dining room tables. Unfortunately, he frightened many of the younger guests to the point of tears. He suffered the added indignity of being scalped when his wig was stolen.

Like most earth shaking inventions, the creation of Patti's 2-inch thick charbroiled pork chop is surrounded by a cloud of controversy.

Mr. Bill maintains the pork chop was the result of trying to make a pork schnitzel, a dish the Tullars had enjoyed while living in Germany. "The first time the 2-inch thick pork chops were ordered from the meat packing company, the computer rejected the order because it thought we had made a mistake in ordering!" laughs Mr. Bill.

Patti, on the other hand, contends the charbroiled delights stemmed from another dish. "When the restaurant first expanded into Patti's 1880's, we served stuffed pork chops. One day a customer ordered the stuffed pork chop, but we were completely out of the cornbread stuffing for the entree. The gentleman persisted, 'I don't care how you cook it, but I want one of those pork chops.' Chip came to the rescue by charbroiling one of the chops— forty five minutes later and black as tar but the customer loved it and we've been doing it ever since!"

Regardless of its beginning, popular opinion confirms that Patti's pork chop is a super success story. More than 200,000 pounds are served a year! Is it any wonder that Patti's was named Kentucky's 1989 Restaurant of the Year by the Kentucky Pork Producers Association.

❀❀❀❀❀❀❀❀

Awards

1994
Paducah Area Chamber of Commerce
Entrepreneur of the Year Award

1994
Blue Chip Enterprise Initiative
Entrepreneur of the Year Award

1995
Chip and Michael Tullar received the
"Kentucky Small Business Persons of the Year,"for 1994
by the U.S. Small Business Administration

1996
Southern Living's Readers Choice Award as one of the top
three small-town restaurants in the South. The only
establishment in Kentucky named on the survey.

❀❀❀❀❀❀❀❀

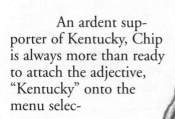

An ardent sup-
porter of Kentucky, Chip
is always more than ready
to attach the adjective,
"Kentucky" onto the
menu selec-

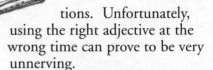

tions. Unfortunately, using the right adjective at the wrong time can prove to be very unnerving.

One evening, Chip ushered a large group of guests into the dining area. When everyone had been seated, Chip, in his usual exuberant manner, welcomed them to Patti's and began to describe the dinner specials. Hastily adding "Kentucky" to the nightly special, he blurted out, "Ladies and gentlemen...tonight our dinner special is Kentucky Fried Chicken."

Needless to say, the dinner guests were quite dumbfounded. The staff, who overheard Chip's slip of the tongue, were rolling with laughter...and poor Chip was left standing in the middle of the dining room trying to figure out just exactly what he had said wrong.

Patti's is a perfect place to host a variety of family reunions, bus tours, group parties and business dinners. Patti's location makes it an easy jaunt from St. Louis, Nashville, Memphis, Evansville, Lexington or Louisville.

Folks may arrive by plane or boat and the friendly staff is always happy to meet them at the Kentucky Dam airport or a local marina. Mr. Bill said, " I got the idea of going to the airport and greeting and picking up people so we got a little van and we set up that routine. It's great to have an airplane but unless you have someplace to go it's sorta boring. This way you could say 'Hey Hazel, let's fly down to Grand Rivers and Bill will pick us up so that we can go eat lunch at Patti's. On the nice days it wouldn't be surprising to have 4 or 5 planes fly in from around the country and we'd pick them up and bring them in to eat. Our record was 45 people in one day from five different states."

The Decor

When the Tullars moved
into the motel in 1975, which has
become Patti's, Bill said "it was furnished in
post war years....ugly, ugly, ugly. Patti always liked
antiques and there are two paintings hanging on the wall
in the downstairs dining room that Patti got for $5.00 a
piece when we moved from California.   So, with that we
started collecting antiques and that pleased Patti because
she loved to go to auctions. Of course that was some 20
years ago but visitors today still enjoy walking through
the dining rooms and admir-
ing here and there
the wonderful
collection of
old tables, pic-
ture frames,
chairs and other
items the family
has collected over
the years from
the great auc-
tions around
western
Kentucky and
Tennessee.

My son, Chip, has a huge heart and loves children. Here he is as Christmas Clown, 1994.

Mr. Bill,

Here's our picture as promised. As you know Patti's has been a part of my life since the late 70's. Your place truly holds a piece of my heart !! I continue to look forward to many more years of returning to Patti's.

Love
Jean Hobbs
9/21/96

One of Bill's many fans.

Appetizers
- & -
Dips

Cocktail Meatballs

2 pounds ground beef
2 eggs
Cracker crumbs
Chopped onions
1/2 cup water

Mix all ingredients, form into bite size meatballs. Place in a baking pan and bake at 350° for 30 minutes. Place meatballs on paper towels to drain.

10-oz. jar grape jelly
1 small bottle chili sauce

Heat jelly and chili sauce until melted. Add meatballs and simmer for 30 minutes. May also use cocktail sausages in place of meatballs or a combination of the two meats.

Patti says this is the greatest ever for entertaining or a catering event.

Patti and Bill make a good working pair. Mr. Bill says it has turned out well all these years because he wanted to be out front visiting with people and Patti wanted to be out back cooking and making up dishes.

Lawana's
Pineapple Cheese Ball

2 8-ounce packages cream cheese
1 small can crushed pineapple
1/4 cup grated green pepper
1 tablespoon grated onion, drained
2 cups chopped pecans

Soften cream cheese and mix in pineapple, pepper and onion.
Add 1 cup of pecans. Refrigerate until chilled. Work into a
ball and roll in rest of nuts. You may also add orange
marmalade or pineapple marmalade over the
top for color and added flavor.

Mike and Lawana Tullar with Arielle and Anna - 1996

Michael T's Bacon Crackers

1/2 cup mayonnaise or salad dressing
1 teaspoon Worcestershire Sauce
1/4 teaspoon salad seasoning
1/8 teaspoon paprika
1 cup shredded Cheddar cheese (about 4 ounces)
4 slices bacon, crisply cooked and crumbled
3 tablespoons chopped salted peanuts
2 tablespoons chopped onions
32 to 36 round crackers

Mix mayonnaise, Worcestershire sauce, salad seasoning and paprika. Stir in cheese, bacon, peanuts and onion. Spread about 1/2 tablespoon mixture over each cracker. Arrange 8 or 9 crackers at a time in circle on plate. Microwave, uncovered, on high (100%) until hot and puffed, about 30 seconds. About 3 dozen appetizers.

Mike with catch of the day down in Key West trying to see how to develop our town into a small Key West style town. It only takes money and time.

Cheese Chili Appetizer

1/2 cup butter
10 eggs
1/2 cup flour
1 teaspoon baking powder
Salt to taste
8-ounce can chopped green chilies
1 pint cottage cheese
1 pound shredded Monterey Jack cheese

Melt butter in 13x9x2" pan. Beat eggs lightly in large bowl. Add flour, baking powder, salt and blend. Add melted butter, chilies, cottage cheese and Monterey Jack cheese. Mix until just blended. Turn batter into pan and bake at 400° for 15 minutes. Reduce to 350°. Bake 35 to 40 minutes longer. Cut into squares and serve hot.

Marian Baugauss, with husband, Frank and clown, Patsy Smith, who was our second general manager and former owner of the Cumberland House. Christmas, 1983.

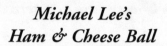

Michael Lee's
Ham & Cheese Ball

2 cups Cheddar cheese
2 cans deviled ham
2 tablespoons Worcestershire sauce
1/4 cup bacon bits
1/4 cup finely minced onion
16-ounce cream cheese
1/2 cup chopped nuts

Let cheese set at room temperature. Mix all ingredients together except nuts. Roll in large ball and roll in nuts. Serve with any type cracker.

Crabmeat and Mushroom Spread

7-1/2 ounce can crabmeat
4-ounce can mushroom stems and pieces,
drained and diced
3 tablespoons sour cream
1/4 teaspoon red pepper sauce
1/4 teaspoon horseradish
1/2 teaspoon salt
1 tablespoon parsley leaves, chopped
1 tablespoon pimento pieces

Mix all together. Chill before serving
with chips or crackers.

Layered Cheese Dome

2 8-ounce packages cream cheese, softened
2 teaspoons lemon juice
1/3 cup grated Parmesan cheese
1 tablespoon cocktail sauce
1/2 cup cream style cottage cheese, drained
1/8 teaspoon onion salt
1/8 teaspoon garlic powder
1/2 cup snipped parsley

In a small mixer bowl, beat together the cream cheese and lemon juice until fluffy. Divide into two portions. To one portion, stir in Parmesan cheese and cocktail sauce. To remaining cream cheese and cottage cheese, onion, salt and garlic powder. Beat until nearly smooth. Stir in parsley. Spoon Parmesan-cream cheese mixture into a lightly oiled 3 cup mold or bowl, spread evenly, leaving a flat surface. Spoon cottage cheese mixture over top. Cover and chill several hours or overnight. Unmold. Garnish with additional parsley, if desired.

Bill and me, our
50th anniversary
picture.

68

Cheese Puffs

*2 cups grated sharp American cheese
1/2 cup soft butter
1 cup sifted all purpose flour
1 teaspoon paprika
48 stuffed olives.*

Blend cheese with butter; stir in flour, salt and paprika. Mix well. Wrap a teaspoon around each olive. Arrange on cookie sheet and freeze. When firm place in 2 or 3 plastic bags and return to freezer. Take from freezer and bake 15 minutes at 400°.

This is a special favorite from Patti's recipe collection. She says it's easy to substitute a cocktail onion if you don't like olives.

Ham Rolls
with Horseradish Cream

8 slices baked ham
8 ounces cream cheese
1/4 teaspoon salt
1 tablespoon horseradish
1 tablespoon orange juice
1/2 orange, sectioned and chopped
8 pimento stuffed olives, chopped

Combine softened cream cheese with remaining ingredients. Spread mixture on ham slices. Roll jelly roll style. Place in pan seam side down. Chill. Cut in 1/2" slices and serve.

So many different people have written about Patti's...even in Tucson and Detroit. Mr. Bill remembers one time he was walking around with his puppets and a man said, "Have you ever been in the *Detroit Ford Press* newspaper in Detroit?" And Bill replied, "No, but I have been in the *Detroit Free Press*" and he reached in to his pocket and pulled out a clipping he had received that very day from a lady in Detroit. She had written to the *Detroit Free Press* praising Patti's.

The gentleman said "I mean *The Ford Times!*" Mr. Bill didn't know *Ford Times* from a gazette, but the next week he got a call from one of the editors with the *Ford Times* and she sent him a form to fill out and some pictures to send in and within 6 months they had written an interesting article about Patti's, complete with pictures! For years later people would come in with the article they had saved for the next time they went to Florida or someplace so that they could stop in at Patti's.

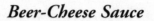

Beer-Cheese Sauce

3/4 cup shredded American cheese
1 tablespoon all purpose flour
1/2 teaspoon dry mustard
Dash paprika
1/3 cup beer
Few dashes bottled hot pepper sauce
3 tablespoons milk

Bring cheese to room temperature. In a small bowl toss cheese with flour, dry mustard and paprika. In a small saucepan heat beer and hot pepper sauce until just warm. gradually add cheese mixture, stirring constantly over medium low heat until cheese is melted and mix is smooth. Stir in milk and heat through. Spoon mixture over Oven Fried Potato Skins. May top with 4 slices bacon, crisp cooked, drained and crumbled.

Oven Fried Potato Skins

Rinse potatoes and bake. Cut in half and scoop out center, leaving a small layer of potato in the shell. Place shells on greased cookie sheet and bake at 350° for 20 minutes or until shells are crisp.

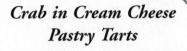

Crab in Cream Cheese Pastry Tarts

1 can crabmeat, rinsed and drained
1 tablespoon lemon juice
1 cup celery, chopped
1/3 cup green onions, chopped
1/2 cup sharp cheese, shredded
1/2 teaspoon Tabasco sauce
1/4 teaspoon seasoned salt

Mix all ingredients and bake in cream cheese pastry.

Cream Cheese Pastry

3 ounces cream cheese
1 cup grated cheddar cheese
1 cup all purpose flour

Mix ingredients together. Form pastry in small tart pans. Fill with crabmeat mixture. Bake at 325° approximately 30 minutes.

Artichoke Dip

1 14-ounce can drained artichoke hearts,
chopped and diced
1 cup mayonnaise
1 cup Parmesan cheese, grated
Garlic powder to taste

Mix ingredients together. Bake at 250° for 30 minutes. Serve
hot with bread or crackers.

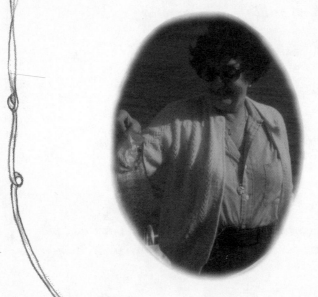

Catch of the day.

Broccoli Dip

2 packages frozen, chopped broccoli
1 small onion, chopped
2-3 ribs celery, chopped
1 6-oz. roll of garlic cheese and
1 can cream of mushroom soup
1 4-oz can mushrooms, drained and chopped
3/4 cup slivered toasted almonds
Chopped pimento
1/2 teaspoon salt
1/4 teaspoon pepper
2 tablespoons butter
1 teaspoon monosodium glutamate
1 teaspoon Worcestershire Sauce
1/4 teaspoon Tabasco

Cook broccoli according to package directions. Let cool in strainer and drain well. Combine all ingredients. Warm thoroughly and serve in a chafing dish.

"It has been a wonderful experience watching Patti's grow. Last time I looked we had folks from 54 different countries sign our guest book. We have entertained the news media from all over the nation, and television stations like TNN," says Mr. Bill.

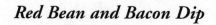

Red Bean and Bacon Dip

3 slices bacon, diced
1 8-ounce can red kidney beans, drained
1 cup sour cream
1 tablespoon chopped green pepper
1 teaspoon instant minced onion
1/4 teaspoon salt
1/8 teaspoon garlic powder
1/8 teaspoon pepper
Tortilla Chips

Place bacon in 1-1/2 quart casserole. Cover with paper towel and microwave on high (100%) for 2 minutes; stir. Cover and microwave until crisp, 1 to 2 minutes longer. Stir in beans; mash with fork. Cover tightly and microwave on high until hot, 2 to 3 minutes. Stir remaining ingredients except tortilla chips into bean mixture. Cover tightly and microwave on high until hot, about 1 minutes. Serve with tortilla chips.

Beverages

- & -

Breads

In addition to the recipes in this section
you'll find the following—

Cider

1 gallon cider
1 cup brown sugar
1 teaspoon whole cloves
1 teaspoon allspice
1 stick cinnamon
1 pinch nutmeg

Mix ingredients together and heat thoroughly.

Cappuccino

1-1/2 cups powdered non-dairy cream
1-1/2 cups chocolate milk dry mix
1 cup instant coffee granules
1-1/2 cups sugar
1/2 teaspoon cinnamon
1/2 teaspoon nutmeg

Mix all ingredients together. Place 3 heaping teaspoons to
coffee mugs; add hot water and stir until dissolved.
Top with whipped cream.

Michael Lee's
Spiced Tea Mix

2 26-ounce jars instant orange-flavored breakfast drink
1 3-ounce jar instant tea
2 8-1/2-ounce packages red cinnamon candies
6-ounce package sweetened lemonade-flavored drink mix
1 cup sugar
2 teaspoons ground cinnamon
2 teaspoons ground nutmeg
2 teaspoons ground cloves
2 teaspoons ground allspice

Combine all ingredients, stirring well. Store in an airtight container. To serve, place 1 tablespoons plus 1 teaspoon mixture in a cup; add 1 cup boiling water, stirring well.
Makes about 14 cups.

Mr. Bill wore overalls around Patti's and they were just the ticket for all the gardening he did. His roses were beautiful and bloomed and bloomed until late into the fall. When Patti bought him a pair of the famous "HeeHaw" overalls from the Nashville Flea Market, they were brightly colored ones that stood out about a mile away. Mr. Bill waited almost a year before he finally got up enough nerve to wear them. Everyone got such a kick out of his overalls.

Michael Lee's Potato Rolls

1 cup sliced potato
3-1/4 to 4 cups all purpose flour
1 package active dry yeast
3 tablespoons butter
2 tablespoons sugar
1 egg
Butter, melted

In saucepan cook potato, covered, in 1 cup water until tender, 15 to 20 minutes. Drain, reserving liquid. Add water, if necessary, to equal 3/4 cup liquid. Mash potato; set aside. In large mixing bowl combine 1 cup of flour and yeast. In saucepan heat the reserved potato liquid, 3 tablespoons butter, sugar and 1-1/2 teaspoons salt just until warm (115-120°); stir constantly. Add to dry mixture; add egg and mashed potato. Beat at low speed of electric mixer for 1/2 minute, scraping sides of bowl constantly. Beat 3 minutes at high speed. By hand, stir in enough of the remaining flour to make a moderately stiff dough. Turn out onto lightly floured surface; knead until smooth. Place in greased bowl; turn once. Cover; let rise in warm place until nearly double. Punch down. Cover; let rest 10 minutes. Roll dough to 1/2 inch thickness. Cut with floured 2-1/2 inch round cutter. Place on greased baking sheets and brush tops with butter. Cover; let rise until nearly double. Bake at 350° for 18-20 minutes. Brush tops with melted butter.
Makes 18 rolls.

Flower Pot Bread

Where did the flower pot bread originate? Well I was familiar with baking in clay since I learned to use it while growing up in Tucson. Later, in Germany, I used a lot of clay dishes, too. So when the restaurant was just beginning, I was lying on my bed one night and an image of bread in a flower pot came to me. The dream didn't give directions or baking instructions, but I decided to try it for myself. I went down in my basement at the big house, where the stove was, and decided to give it a whirl. It was winter and we weren't open, so I had plenty of time to try all my experiments.

I found that by taking yeast bread, the kind that rises once, so you don't have to punch down, it might work. It wouldn't work, of course, if you had to punch it down. I had to figure out how to season the pots, so I soaked them in water to fill up the porous clay holes and then put a hard grease coating—Crisco or lard, inside and out and everywhere. If the oven had a pilot light, I'd put the pots in there and leave them overnight or turn the oven down really low to seal the pots. Then I'd grease my ball of dough and grease the pot, let the bread rise and bake at 300 to 325 degrees. It will get too brown if it's cooked at any higher temperature. Often one part would get too brown, the other, underdone. It's necessary to bake it long enough so it's not doughy and it will come out of the pots. For home baking, don't wash the pots in soap and water or the grease will come off!

While working at the pier restaurant, I baked all the bread. I would have big, tall proofers all over the place. Of course I would need help in lifting those huge trays of pots filled with bread — that's why I had three boys — to help lift everything!

Season Flowerpots

Clean pots thoroughly; place on baking
sheet. Wipe with shortening thoroughly. Bake at
275° for 30 minutes. Remove from oven; cover with
shortening all over again while hot. When pots cool coat with
nonstick cooking spray all over again, then place dough into
pots. If you have a gas stove, you may leave
in oven overnight.

*Chip and Mike, 1996. President and Vice President of Tullar
Enterprises. They are the boys who enjoy eating.*

Banana Nut Bread

2 sticks margarine
2 cups sugar
4 egg yolks
2 tablespoons water with 2 tablespoons soda, dissolved
6 large bananas, best when very ripe
4 cups flour
4 egg whites
1-1/2 cup nuts

Mix margarine, sugar, egg yolks, soda with water and bananas.
Beat well. Add flour and mix well. Beat egg whites and fold
in. Bake at 350° for 1-1/4 hours. Makes two small pans or
one large pan. Can be baked in a Bundt or tube pan.

A tip from Patti is to throw the brown bananas in the freezer,
skin and all, when they become too ripe. They are easy to store
this way and you'll always have them on hand when you are
ready to bake banana bread.

Cranberry Orange Bread

2 cups flour
1 cup sugar
1-1/2 teaspoons baking powder
1/2 teaspoon baking soda
1/2 teaspoon salt
2 tablespoons vegetable oil
Grated rind and juice of 1 orange and
enough water to make 3/4 cups*
1 egg, beaten
1 cup raw cranberries, halved
1/2 cup chopped nuts

Heat oven to 350°. Grease one loaf pan. Measure flour. Blend dry ingredients. Mix together the oil, orange rind, juice and egg. Add to dry ingredients and stir only enough to moisten. Fold in cut up cranberries and nuts. Pour into pan. Bake one hour. Cool thoroughly before slicing.
   *May also use 1 tablespoon frozen orange juice concentrate and 3/4 cup reconstituted orange juice.

Whenever a festival or local parade took place, Mr. Bill and Patti loaded up the pig and participated in the event. "Anyway we could spread the word of Patti's, we did," says Mr. Bill, who has always been a marketeer.

Michael Lee's
Carrot-Wheat Muffins

3/4 cup whole wheat flour
2 teaspoons baking powder
1/2 teaspoon baking soda
1 teaspoon pumpkin pie spice
2 tablespoons wheat germ, toasted
1 cup grated carrots
1/2 cup raisins
1 egg, slightly beaten
1 cup milk
1/4 cup honey
1/4 cup vegetable oil
1-1/2 cups morsels of wheat bran cereal

Combine flour, baking powder, soda, pie spice, wheat germ, grated carrots and raisins in a medium bowl; set aside. Combine egg and remaining ingredients in a small bowl; stir well and let stand for 3 minutes. Make a well in center of flour mixture. Add cereal mixture to dry ingredients, stirring just until moistened. Spoon wheat mixture into greased muffin pans, filling three-fourths full. Bake at 400° for 18 to 20 minutes. Makes 12 muffins.

Note: After baking, be sure to remove muffins from the pans so that the bottoms of the muffins won't get soggy.

Patti's Strawberry Donuts

Fashion yeast bread dough into a round donut, and cover a fresh moist strawberry with powdered sugar and place it in the middle of your doughnut. Fry in a deep fat fryer until it rises to the surface. Roll in a mixture of cinnamon and sugar and serve hot.

Another delicious way to greet the morning is with my Bran Muffins. I love the convenience of these muffins, because you can make the batter and keep it for up to six weeks in the refrigerator. When you get up in the morning, pour the batter into a muffin pan, pop into the oven and fresh, hot muffins are ready 25 minutes later!

Bran Muffins

1 20-ounce box of raisin bran
3 cups sugar
5 cups plain flour
5 teapoons baking soda
2 teaspoons salt
4 eggs, slightly beaten
1 cup margarine, melted
5 cups buttermilk

Mix the bran flakes, sugar, flour, soda and salt by hand. In a separate bowl mix the eggs, margarine and buttermilk. Make a well in the bran mixture, and pour the egg mixture into it. Stir just enough to mix well. Pour into greased muffin pans.
Bake in a 300 degree oven for 20 - 25 minutes.
Makes 36 muffins.

Chip became deacon of St. Peter's of the Lakes
Episcopal Church, 1996.

Chip's
Pumpkin-Pecan Loaves

1 cup margarine, melted
1 cup granulated sugar
1 cup brown sugar, packed
4 eggs
1 16-ounce can pumpkin
2-3/4 cups flour
1 tablespoon pumpkin pie spice
2 teaspoons baking powder
1 teaspoon baking soda
1 teaspoon salt
1 cup chopped pecans, optional

Heat oven to 350°. Combine margarine and sugars. Add eggs, one at a time, mixing well after each addition. Blend in pumpkin. Add combined dry ingredients; mix only until moistened. Stir in nuts, if using. Pour into 2 greased and floured 9x5" loaf pans. Bake at 350°, 1 hour and 10 minutes or until wooden pick inserted in center comes out clean. Cool 10 minutes; remove from pan.

Lawana's
Apple Date Dream

2 cups sifted all purpose flour
1 cup sugar
1-1/2 teaspoons baking soda
1 teaspoon salt
1 teaspoon cinnamon
2 slightly beaten eggs
1 21-ounce can apple pie filling
1/2 cup cooking oil
1 teaspoon vanilla
1 cup chopped dates
1/4 cup chopped walnuts

Sift together flour, sugar, soda, salt and cinnamon. Combine eggs, pie filling, oil and vanilla; stir into flour mixture and mix well. Stir in dates and nuts. Pour into greased and floured 8-3/4x13-1/2" baking dish. Bake in 350° oven for 40-45 minutes.

On dieting and fat free, low-cal foods...Julia Child has the best outlook on dieting and the flavor of foods. She says just don't eat so much, take smaller portions of the foods you like. Don't sacrifice the taste or flavor.

88

Gail's
Butterscotch Pecan Rolls

1 3.5-ounce package butterscotch pudding mix
1 package frozen round dough yeast rolls
1 cup dark brown sugar
1 stick butter or margarine
Chopped pecans

Spray Bundt pan with cooking spray. Place frozen rolls in Bundt pan. Pour dry butterscotch pudding mix over frozen rolls. Sprinkle brown sugar over top. Melt and pour butter over rolls. Sprinkle with chopped pecans. Let stand out on counter top overnight. Rolls will thaw and rise. Bake for 20 minutes at 350°. Cool for 25 minutes in pan before turning out.

Patti Playing Bridge

I have played bridge for years and years and first learned while I was enrolled at the University of Arizona. It's a great way to meet new friends. My sorority sisters and I could always find a foursome for a "pickup game" at noon, between classes at the sorority house . When I moved to Grand Rivers I was certain I was the only bridge player in town. So, missing my wonderful card-playing days, I drove to Paducah, some 25 miles away, where I enjoyed duplicate bridge. From the daughter of one of my bridge-playing friends comes this recipe above, which I still enjoy.

Patti's
Raisin Ginger Muffins

2 cups all-purpose flour
1-1/2 teaspoons baking soda
1/4 teaspoon salt
1-1/2 teaspoons ground ginger
1/3 cup butter or margarine
1 cup molasses
1/2 cup buttermilk
1 egg, slightly beaten
1/2 cup chopped pecans
1/2 cup raisins

Combine first 4 ingredients in a medium bowl; set aside.
Combine butter and molasses in a small saucepan; cook over
medium heat until the butter melts. Remove from heat. Make
a well in center of flour mixture. Add molasses mixture, buttermilk and egg, stirring just until ingredients are moistened.
Stir in chopped pecans and raisins. Spoon mixture into greased
muffin pans, filling three-fourths full. Bake at 325° for 18
minutes or until done. Makes 18 muffins.

Kimberly's
Pecan Muffins

1-1/2 cups all purpose flour
2 teaspoons baking powder
1/4 teaspoon salt
1/2 cup firmly packed brown sugar
Pinch of allspice
1 egg, slightly beaten
1/3 cup milk
1/4 cup maple-flavored syrup
1/2 cup butter or margarine, melted
1 cup coarsely chopped pecans
1 teaspoon vanilla extract
1/4 cup sugar
1/4 teaspoon ground cinnamon
1/4 cup butter or margarine, melted

Combine first 5 ingredients in a medium bowl; make a well in center of mixture. Combine egg milk, syrup and 1/2 cup butter; add to dry ingredients, stirring until just moistened. Stir in pecans and vanilla. Fill paper-lined muffin pans two thirds full. Bake at 400° for 15 to 20 minutes. Combine sugar and cinnamon. Dip tops of warm muffins in remaining 1/4 cup butter, then sugar mixture.
Makes 12 muffins.

Zamma's Banana Bread

2 sticks butter, softened
2 cups sugar
2 tablespoons water
2 teaspoons baking soda
4 cups flour
4 eggs, separated
6 large ripe bananas, mashed
1-1/2 cups chopped nuts

Cream butter and sugar. Dissolve baking soda in water and add to sugar mixture. Stir in flour, egg yolks, bananas and nuts. Beat egg whites until stiff; fold into batter. Pour into greased and floured loaf pans.   Bake at 350° for 1 hour or until wooden pick comes out clean.

Patti's Soups - & - Salads

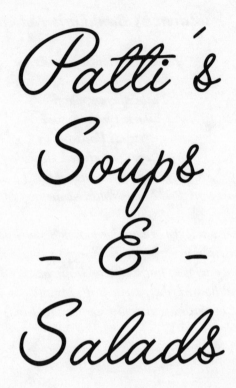

In addition to the recipes in this section
you'll find the following—

Patti's Chili page 38

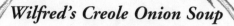

Wilfred's Creole Onion Soup

1/2 pound unsalted butter
3 medium onions, thinly sliced
1/2 cup all purpose flour
2 quarts chicken stock
1 small bay leaf
3 ounces Cheddar cheese, shredded
1/2 cup dry white wine
Salt and freshly ground black pepper to taste

Melt butter in a large heavy saucepan and sauté sliced onions briefly. Just before they become transparent, add flour and stir well. Add stock, bay leaf, cheese and wine. Stir over low heat until cheese is thoroughly melted, then simmer for about 15 minutes. Correct seasoning with salt and pepper and serve immediately. Serves 6 to 8.

53rd anniversary, 1996 with the whole Tullar family. Left to right,
Michael Lee, Cousin Pam, my brother Ron, his wife Mary Ann,
Ronnie, Bill, Chip, myself, Wilfred, Kim, Dohnte.

Michael's Étoufeé

2 quarts water
1/2 pound shrimp base
6 cups tomato sauce
6 cups diced tomatoes, drained
1 tablespoon garlic powder
1/2 tablespoon dried basil
1/2 tablespoon dried oregano
1/2 tablespoon dried thyme
1/2 teaspoon red pepper
1/2 teaspoon black pepper
1/2 teaspoon white pepper
1 cup salad oil
1 cup flour
1 cup celery, chopped
1 cup onions, chopped

Put water and shrimp base in large pot to heat until hot. In large sauté pan, combine salad oil and flour, making roux. Stir continuously until dark brown. DO NOT BURN. Once roux is dark brown, turn off heat and add celery and onions. Stir until combined. Combine the rest of ingredients into heated broth and stir.

Cream of Beefy Mushroom Soup

1 can Cream of Mushroom Soup
1 can milk
1 ounce package au jus mix, or 1 or 2 bouillon cubes
depending on how
beefy a flavor you want

Mix all ingredients and heat thoroughly. May add 1/2 box
frozen chopped broccoli, thawed, for Cream of Broccoli
Mushroom Soup.

For years Bill would pick up the tourists from marinas and airports in his Patti's
Jitney. Most of the time Calvin Swine rode up front and the
tourists in the rumble seat.

Patti's Gazpacho

1/2 cup chopped onion
1-1/2 cups peeled, chopped cucumbers
1 cup chopped green peppers
1 2-pound can peeled Italian tomatoes
1 cups consommé
1/4 cup lemon juice
3/4 cup V-8 vegetable juice
1/2 cup Snap-E-Tom
1/4 cup olive oil
1-1/4 teaspoons salt
1/8 teaspoon each pepper, tarragon, basil, oregano,
marjoram, thyme and parsley
1 clove garlic, minced

Combine all ingredients in large bowl. Put 1-2 cups in a
blender at a time until all ingredients are blending to a pour
consistency. Chill well. This may also be served hot or as an
aspic. To prepare the aspic, dissolve 1 tablespoon gelatin in 1/4
cup tomato juice over hot water. Add this to each pint of
gazpacho and chill overnight to mold.

Pistachio Salad

1 large package pistachio pudding mix
1 large container whipped cream
1 large can crushed pineapple, drained
2 cups nuts

Add pistachio pudding mix to whipped cream; mix in pineapple and nuts.   Cool until ready to serve.

Patti's Tuna Salad

2-1/2-ounce can of chunk tuna, drained
1/4 cup chopped celery
1 tablespoon sweet pickle relish
1 hard boiled egg, diced
Dash of black pepper
1/2 cup mayonnaise
Sliced green grapes and toasted almonds optional -
Nice if you want it to be special

Mix all ingredients and refrigerate until ready to serve.
Wonderful stuffed in summer fresh tomatoes.

Add cream cheese to mixture for tasty wonderful delight that
leaves guests wondering what is that unique taste
I'm sensing.

Crunchy Rotelle Salad

1 cup cooked rotelle or wagon wheels
1 cup frozen English peas, thawed and drained
8 ounces cooked ham, cubed
1/2 cup chopped celery
1/4 cup chopped radishes
1/4 cup chopped green pepper
1/4 cup sweet pickle salad cubes
1/2 cup mayonnaise
1/4 cup sweet pickle juice

Combine all ingredients and chill before serving.

Those who enter to buy support me.
Those who come to flatter, please me.
Those who complain teach me how I
may please others so more will come.
Only those hurt me who are displeased
but do not complain.
They refuse me permission to correct my errors
and thus improve my service.

from Marshall Field,
Business Leader & Philanthropist

Marinated
Artichoke Salad

1 green pepper, thinly sliced
1 small onion, thinly sliced
8-1/2-ounce can artichoke hearts, drained
1/2 cup diced celery
1 cucumber, unpeeled and thinly sliced
1 cup cubed mozzarella cheese
1/2 pound fresh mushrooms, sliced
1 tablespoon salt
1/4 teaspoon pepper
1/4 teaspoon dillweed
2 slices bacon, cooked and crumbled

Marinade:
1/2 cup salad oil
3 tablespoons cider vinegar
1 tablespoon lemon juice
1 tablespoon dry mustard
1/2 teaspoon salt
1/8 teaspoon pepper

Combine first 10 ingredients. Toss with marinade. Chill
several hours. Garnish with bacon. Serve on fresh
tossed spinach leaves as salad course.

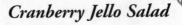

Cranberry Jello Salad

1 16-ounce can cranberry sauce
1 15-ounce can crushed pineapple,
(drained, reserving juice)
2 3-ounce packages raspberry jello
2 cups hot liquid (juice and water)
1 cup sour cream
1 cup chopped nuts, toasted

Mix cranberry sauce and 1 cup of the hot liquid until smooth.
Dissolve both packages of jello in 1 cup boiling liquid. Add
cranberry mix and pineapple to gelatin. Pour half the mixture
in a 9x13" pan and chill until firm. Spread sour cream and
remaining mixture to pan. Chill. Sprinkle with toasted nuts
before serving.

Green Salad

1 large can crushed pineapple
1/4 cup sugar
1 large box lime jello
1 large cake cream cheese
1 small Cool Whip

Boil pineapple and sugar for 1 minutes. Blend powdered jello
into cream cheese. Let jell a little. Add pineapple with an
electric beater. Fold in Cool Whip. Place in mold which
has been lightly covered with mayonnaise. Refrigerate
until ready to serve.

Cucumber Salad

4 peeled and sliced cucumbers
1 onion, sliced
1-1/2 cups salad dressing
1/2 cup sugar
Vinegar until tart
Salt and pepper to taste

Mix dressing, sugar, vinegar, salt and pepper together. Add cucumbers and onions. Let stand overnight. Keeps well for two weeks or more.

Lawana's Southwestern Three Bean Salad

1 16-ounce can black beans, drained and rinsed
1 15-ounce can pinto beans or black-eyed peas, drained and rinsed
1 19-ounce can chickpeas, drained and rinsed
1/2 small Vidalia onion, halved and thinly sliced
1/2 cup chopped cilantro
2-3 chipotle peppers packed in adobo sauce, drained and finely chopped
3 tablespoons cider vinegar
2 tablespoons olive oil
Salt and freshly ground black pepper to taste.

In a large bowl, combine all ingredients. Toss until well mixed. This salad can be prepared ahead and stored, covered in the refrigerator for up to 2 days. Serves 6.

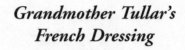

Grandmother Tullar's
French Dressing

4 teaspoons salt
3 cups vinegar
1 cup water
6 cups sugar
4 cups ketchup
1/2 cup dry mustard
8 tablespoons grated onion
2-3/4 tablespoons paprika
3 cups salad oil

Mix first 8 ingredients together and slowly beat in the salad oil.
Refrigerate.

This is the recipe Patti's Restaurant uses for their French Dressing.

Ronnie's
Cajun Hot Potato Salad

7 to 8 potatoes
3 to 4 eggs
1 cup mayonnaise
2 tablespoons mustard
4 green onions, sliced
1 tablespoon butter
1/3 cup milk
Cayenne pepper and salt to taste

Peel and dice potatoes. Put in large saucepan. Add eggs, boil until potatoes are tender; drain and run under cold water. Peel eggs. In large bowl, add butter and potatoes. Mash; add milk, mayonnaise, mustard. Mix with wooden spoon. Add eggs, onion, cayenne pepper and salt. Salad should be smooth like mashed potatoes. Serves 4-6 people.

This is a wonderful treat with any picnic.

Chip Tullar's Super Bowl Party

Chip loves to entertain. Until recently he had never even been to a Super Bowl Party; he always worked and never had time— but this year he decided he would celebrate this event so many folks talked about. Chip asked a woman in the check out lines at Walmart, "what do you prepare?" She said "chips and dip."The next day he ventured to the IGA in Grand Rivers and again asked, " what do you serve at a Super Bowl Party?" They told him, "oh, the usual— hot dogs, popcorn, chips and dip."

Well, Chip has never been one to entertain friends in an ordinary way—he always wants to"do it up", make the event "something special." So that's exactly what he did—he pulled foods off the shelves of the store and loaded the shopping cart and returned home where he pulled out his sterling silverware, fine china dishes, all the crystal and candlesticks he could find and set a beautiful table in the dining room of his hundred-year old house!

In the kitchen he threw together a can of pearl potatoes, a head of cabbage, frozen carrots and onions in a pot with water, a can of chicken noodle soup and boiled them down. For his pork roast he mixed together teriyaki sauce, chablis wine and pork chop seasoning, poured it over top and baked it. His appetizers were ramekins made of bacon covering pearl onions along with stuffed eggs.

His recipe for salad follows plus a quick and easy dessert recipe which all his guests insisted they could not possibly hold after the delicious dinner, but which each and every one gobbled up in a flash.They all had great fun and agreed it was the best Super Bowl Party ever, even if it was their very first. No wonder the guests are already looking forward to celebrating this "sports event" in 1998.

Chip's Super
Bowl Party Salad

1 jar of 3-bean salad in oil
1 jar of artichoke hearts in oil
1 stalk celery, chopped
1 cup broccoli, chopped
1 cup cauliflower, chopped
1 small container pimento cheese spread
Red lettuce leaves
Spinach leaves
Lettuce leaves

Mix together the 3 bean salad with the jar of artichoke hearts, adding all the oil of both jars. Chop celery, broccoli and cauliflower and add to mixture. Refrigerate and chill for several hours. For individual servings, place mixture on a bed of red lettuce and spinach leaves, then dollop pimento cheese spread to the side for color and special taste. Serves 8.

Entrees, Beef, Chicken & Seafood

In addition to the recipes in this section
you'll find the following—

Chicken Enchiladas page 43
Ronnie's Favorite Pot Roast page 28

Florence Perry

I remember my mother, Florence Perry, as a wonderful cook! My younger brother, Ronald, and I especially loved mother's Swiss steak. He now lives on a cattle ranch in Arizona near Tucson on the Nogales-Mexican border. It is so far out in the desert that they have to generate their own electricity and are without telephones. When the Perry's hold their yearly cattle round-up, the Swiss Steak recipe is in high demand.

Patti's Mother's Swiss Steak

Using a meat mallet, pound flour into the round steak until the steak thins slightly and is covered with flour. Brown the steak in a little bit of hot oil. Add one can of whole tomatoes, one chopped onion, chopped carrots and other vegetables as desired. Add one cup of water or beef stock and cook in a covered Dutch oven for several hours until tender. Thicken the broth left in the oven after cooking with flour or corn starch to make gravy.

Mom did not like onions, and I remember when she used to cook meatloaf there would be a toothpick stuck in the middle, dividing the onion side of the loaf from the non-onion side!

Bill Tullar

Chip says that one of his dad's greatest wishes is to be seen on the cover of *USA Today*, walking his beloved designer pig, Calvin Swine to the local grocery in Grand Rivers. For that's exactly what they did each summer morning, take a walk— a pig dressed up and on a leash and a grey-bearded gentleman strolling the big city streets of Grand Rivers, KY, population—about 350. "Go for it , Dad, one dream to go."

Where did all the animals originate? Why, Mr. Bill, of course. "One day I was talking to a customer and he said he had a llama he would give us. Well, we had to build a pen and house for it and did, but then the llama got sick. I called the owner and the vet and they both came but the llama died. We sent it for an autoposy and it turned out the llama died of ulcers and a broken heart. He was lonely. So the customer said he had the llama's son and would sell him to us. Next thing I know we're buying a goat to keep the llama company so he wouldn't be lonesome. Well, one animal led to another. The son was called Colonel after his dad and still resides at Patti's today."

Ronnie's Oven-Baked
Pork Baby Back Ribs
with Small Potatoes
and Mustard Greens

3 pounds baby back ribs
3 pounds small thin skinned potatoes, scrubbed
3 cups chicken broth
1 pound greens, tough stems trimmed off
1/3 cup barbecue sauce

In two 10 x 15 inch metal pans, divide ribs, carved side up.
Pour 1-1/2 cups broth over ribs in each pan. Tightly cover
with foil. Bake at 400° for one hour. Turn ribs over; place
potatoes around them. Seal pans and cook until potatoes are
done. Put potatoes on platter. Keep warm. Drain juices into
bowl. Place ribs back in oven until brown (high heat). Add
barbecue sauce, meat juices and greens. Stir over high heat until
greens are wilted. Serves 6 to 8.

Lasagna

Sauce:
1/4 cup olive oil
4 tablespoons butter
1 clove garlic, peeled and crushed
1 pound pork sausage, crumbled
1/2 pound loin of pork, finely ground
1 pound ground beef
6 to 8 sprigs parsley, finely chopped
1-1/2 teaspoons dried basil
Pinch thyme
Pinch oregano
Salt and freshly ground pepper
1/2 cup dry red wine
2-1/2 tablespoons tomato paste
1 17-ounce can peeled tomatoes

2-1/2 pounds lasagna
2 cups ricotta cheese
1 egg yolk
Butter
1 cup Pecorino cheese, grated
1 cup Parmesan cheese, grated
1/4 pound Mozzarella cheese, diced rather small

Make the sauce first: Heat the oil and butter in a large, heavy
saucepan.   Add the garlic.   When it is brown, discard.
Add the sausage. when it begins to brown, add the
pork. Sauté over moderate heat until brown.
Add the beef, give the mixture

*a good stir and cook
for another 15 minutes. Stir
in all the herbs, salt and pepper to
taste and continue to cook, stirring
occasionally, for 10 minutes. Stir in wine and
cook until it has boiled away. Mix the tomato paste
with 1/2 cup of warm water and stir into the sauce.
Cook another 15 minutes. Add the tomatoes and cook until
the sauce thickens and the tomatoes are dissolving into the
sauce, approximately 40 minutes longer. Cook the lasagna,
drain carefully and rinse under cold water. Beat the ricotta
and egg yolk until smooth. Brush the bottom of a 9x14x2"
dish with melted butter. Layer with half the lasagna, half the
cheese, half the sauce. Repeat the layers. Bake in a preheated
325° oven for 15 to 20 minutes or until piping hot through.
Serves 8 to 10.*

*Can't use too much of the cheeses in any proportion, based on
how rich you want the dish to be. I personally recommend lots
of cheese.*

Sweet and Sour Ribs

2 sides (5 to 6 pounds total) pork spareribs
1 8-ounce can tomato sauce
2/3 cup dry Sherry or apple juice
2/3 cup honey
1/4 cup cider vinegar
1/4 cup soy sauce
3 cloves garlic, minced
2 tablespoons minced onion
1 teaspoon salt
1 teaspoon celery seed
1 teaspoon Worcestershire sauce
Dash pepper
Dash liquid hot pepper seasoning
1/2 teaspoon ground ginger

Put meat in single layers of 2 large roasting pans. Place in a
450° oven for 30 minutes. Drain and discard the fat; cut ribs
apart into serving sized pieces and combine in one pan about
12x18". Reset oven at 350°. Meanwhile, in a pan combine
the tomato sauce with all of the remaining ingredients.
Simmer uncovered about 20 minutes, then pour over ribs in
baking pan; cover tightly with foil and put into a 350° oven for
40 minutes. Remove foil, baste ribs with sauce and bake
uncovered for 40 minutes longer, basting often. Makes
about 6 servings.

Ronnie's Smothered Pork Chops

4 pork chops
Salt and pepper to taste
Flour
1 tablespoon oil
1 large onion, chopped
1 clove garlic, minced
1/2 teaspoon chopped parsley
1/8 teaspoon crushed thyme
1 bay leaf

Season pork chops to taste with salt and pepper. Lightly dust with flour. Heat oil in heavy non-stick skillet. Fry chops until golden brown on both sides. Remove chops from pan and keep warm. Add onion and garlic to skillet drippings and sauté until tender. Stir in 1 teaspoon flour and brown. Return chops to pan. Add water to cover chops, approximately 3 cups. Add parsley, thyme and bay leaf. Simmer, uncovered, over low heat until chops are tender, about 30 to 40 minutes. Remove chops to serving plate. Reduce sauce in skillet to desired consistency. Adjust seasonings to taste. Serve over chops. Makes 4 servings.

You can add cabbage and simmer together with pork chops. Excellent together. You can't use too much seasoning either. You can add cajun seasoning for creole version.

Ronnie's
Smothered Cabbage
& Pork Ribs

2 to 3 heads of cabbage
6 pork chops or country style ribs
1/4 cup corn oil
1-1/2 cups water
Red or black pepper, salt and garlic to taste

In large pot, chop or dice heads of cabbage. Add meat, oil, water, and seasonings. Cook over medium heat until meat is done. Serve with rice.

Ronnie says "In our family we usually put the cabbage on top of the rice. This recipe is easy and only takes about 45 minutes to 1 hour. You could also use pork chunks instead of ribs or chops."

The buying crew at dinner in Dallas, 1995 This gang of smiling people bring you all the gifts we sell in our settlement. Left to right, Karen, Marian, Betty, myself, Chip.

Secret Weapon

Any size pot roast, chuck roast, etc., not too lean
1 package Lipton Onion Soup Mix
10-1/4 ounce can cream of mushroom soup, undiluted
1/2 teaspoon black pepper

Place roast on large piece of aluminum foil. Sprinkle with pep-
per, spread with mushroom soup. Evenly spread onion soup
mix on top of mushroom soup then seal foil tightly and place in
shallow baking pan. Bake at 250° for at least 6 hours. Frozen
roast may be used without thawing but allow to cook at least 8
hours. Makes its own rich gravy.

My extended family of wonderful friends. Left to right, Michael Lee, Rick, Charlie, Mike,
Chip, myself and Irene from Lite Side Cafe across from Patti's. Eat with us or die!

Meatloaf for Christmas

My sister-in-law, Mary Ann Perry, gave me her favorite recipe for meatloaf many years ago. I adore meatloaf, but never seemed to have a chance to make it for my family. One year I decided it would be a nice change from the traditional turkey to serve it to my family for Christmas. This was back when we were living in the big house in Grand Rivers, and as there was only a wood stove there, I had to cook Christmas dinner at the restaurant, running back and forth between the house and the restaurant in the midst of pouring down rain.

How was the meatloaf received by the family? Suffice it to say that the children were aghast. Even if the meatloaf did have cheese and ham in it, it was a meatloaf instead of a turkey. And to top it all, what with the rain and the having to run back and forth, the meatloaf was overdone. The children never got over it.

Aunt Mary Ann's Sicilian Meatloaf is a delicious variation on the traditional dish, and with the ham and cheese makes a beautiful presentation when cut and served on the plate. Just don't serve it for Christmas dinner!

Aunt Mary Ann's
Sicilian Meat Roll

2 eggs, beaten
3/4 cup soft bread crumbs (1 slice bread)
1/2 cup tomato juice
2 tablespoons parsley, snipped
1/2 teaspoon oregano
1/4 teaspoon salt
1/4 teaspoon pepper
1 small clove garlic, minced
2 pounds ground beef
8 thin slices boiled ham
6 ounces (1-1/2 cups) shredded mozzarella cheese
3 slices of mozzarella cheese, halved diagonally

Combine first 8 ingredients, add meat and mix. Pat meat mixture onto a 12 x 10 inch rectangle piece of aluminum foil. Put ham slices on meat, leaving margins around edge. Spread shredded cheese over ham. Start rolling from short end, using foil to lift like you were making a roll cake, taking foil off as you roll. Seal edges and ends. Place rolled seam side down in 13 x 9 inch baking pan. Bake at 350 degrees for 1 hour 15 minutes or until done. (Will be pink). Place cheese wedges over top of roll and melt for 5 minutes more.

Michael Lee's
Cold Pork Loin

1 6-pound pork loin roast rubbed generously
with thyme and dry mustard
1/2 cup dry sherry
1/2 cup soy sauce
2 tablespoons ground ginger
3 cloves garlic, pressed
8 ounces currant or apple jelly
1 tablespoon soy sauce
2 tablespoons dry sherry
Orange slices, optional

Combine the 1/2 cup sherry, soy sauce, ginger and garlic and
pour over roast. Marinate overnight. Remove meat from marinade; reserve marinade. Bake at 325° for 25 minutes per
pound or until meat thermometer reaches 175°, basting often
with marinade. Melt jelly over medium heat. Add soy sauce
and the 2 tablespoons of sherry, mixing well. Cool. Place roast
on a rack in a shallow pan. Spoon glaze over roast. As mixture
runs off into pan, repeat to build up a coating. Slice and serve
cold or hot, garnished with orange slices. Wonderful for
cold sandwich tray with any bread compliment.

Kidney Bean and Cheese Casserole

6 slices bacon, diced
1 large onion, chopped fine
1 clove garlic, chopped fine
1 15-ounce can tomato sauce
2 tablespoons chili powder
1 teaspoon salt
3 kidney beans, drained
1 pound Monterey Jack or Cheddar cheese, diced

Place bacon in a cold skillet and fry over moderate heat until barely crisp. Lift to a heavy saucepan with 2 tablespoons of fat. Stir in onions and garlic; cook until soft. Stir in tomato sauce, chili powder and beans. Cover and cook over very low heat for 1 hour. Stir in the cheese and cook until cheese is melted. Serve immediately.

The Tullar Family & Owners of Patti's.
Me, Bill with Arielle, Lawana with Anna,
Michael Lee, Chip, Michael T.- 1996.

Beef Bourguignonne

3 pounds lean beef (sirloin, chuck or round)
2-1/2 cups Burgundy wine
1/8 teaspoon garlic powder
1/8 teaspoon thyme
1/2 bay leaf
1/4 cup oil
3 tablespoons flour
1 package onion soup mix
1-1/2 cups water
5 small carrots, cooked and cut into 1 inch chunks
1 8-ounce can small onions
1 4-ounce can mushrooms or 12 fresh mushrooms
sautéed in butter

Cut beef into 1-1/2 inch cubes. Combine 2 cups Burgundy, garlic powder, thyme and bay leaf. Pour over beef; let stand 2 hours or longer. Drain beef, saving the juice marinade. Pat cubes dry. Heat oil in skillet; add beef. Brown on all sides. Put beef in casserole. Stir flour into oil remaining in skillet. Add Burgundy marinade, onion soup mix and water. Cook, stirring constantly, until it boils. Pour over beef. Cover and bake in 300° oven for 2 hours or until beef is very tender. Add cooked carrots, drained onions and mushrooms. Add vegetables and 1/2 cup Burgundy to casserole with beef. Bake 15 minutes longer. Makes 6 to 8 servings.

Baked Spaghetti

8 ounces spaghetti
2 tablespoons butter or margarine
2 pounds ground beef
2 8-ounce cans tomato sauce
2 tablespoons flour
2 teaspoons salt
2 cups cottage cheese
1 cup sour cream
1/4 cup chopped green onions
1/4 cup chopped ripe olives

Cook spaghetti according to package directions and drain. Melt
butter in large skillet. Add meat and brown slowly, breaking up
during cooking.   Drain off excess drippings. Add tomato sauce,
flour and 1 teaspoon salt. Simmer for 20 minutes. Add
remaining ingredients and cook an additional 10 minutes.
Place half of the spaghetti in a 9x13 baking dish; top with layer
of sauce. Repeat layers and bake in 350° oven for 30 minutes.
Let stand for 10 minutes before serving.

From our Germany days. This recipe was given by a friend who
lived upstairs.

Carol June Pizza

1 Chef Boyardee packaged pizza mix
(with sauce and cheese)
1 pound ground beef
1 onion, chopped
1 green pepper, chopped
Salt and pepper to taste
1/2 small can tomatoes and chilies
1/4 stick Cracker Barrel sharp cheese, grated
1 package grated mozzarella cheese

Prepare packaged pizza mix with sauce and cheese according to package instructions. Brown ground beef. Season to personal taste with garlic and/or onion powder. Add onion, green pepper, salt and pepper. Spread over pizza, mainly around edges. Spread remaining ingredients over top. Bake in 450° oven until brown on edges and cheese is melted.

Rudy's Caldillo

1 round steak with fat removed
6-8 medium sized potatoes
1 pint tomatoes
6-8 cloves garlic (do not substitute garlic powder)
1 small onion, diced
1/2 teaspoon cumin
1/2 teaspoon pepper
Seasoned salt to taste

Cut steak into bite sized pieces; quick fry, at high temperature, in iron skillet to brown. Cut potatoes and tomatoes into small pieces. Add to browned meat. Stir in garlic which has been crushed, onion, cumin, pepper and seasoned salt. Add water to cover mixture. Cook at low heat for 4 hours or until potatoes are soft and disintegrating.

A breakfast suggestion for leftover Caldillo: Fry corn tortilla, top with fried egg and cover with Caldillo. Delicious!!!

I insist on using only Kikoman soy sauce at the restaurant. You can also add a little Kentucky bourbon whiskey, too, for a great tenderizer. Try our special Pork Chop Seasoning as a substitute for salt and pepper.

Madonna's Pizza Casserole

1 pound ground beef
1 jar or can spaghetti sauce
1 container crescent rolls
3 cups Cheddar cheese, grated
3 cups mozzarella cheese, grated

Brown ground beef and drain. Add the spaghetti sauce and
cook over low heat. Layer Cheddar cheese in the bottom of a
9x13 coated pan, then add the ground beef mixture, then layer
the mozzarella cheese. For the top, spread the crescent rolls
across the top of the dish. Bake at 350° for 15 minutes or
until golden brown.

*My sons, Chip and Michael Lee along with Sadie, 1996. Chip is president of
the company and president of Kentucky State Restaurant Associations, 1997.
Michael Lee is our guy Friday. He does everything that needs doing.
Michael Lee is our adopted son.*

Chicken Cannelloni

3/4 cup celery, thinly sliced
1/2 cup carrots, thinly sliced
1/2 cup mushrooms, sliced
1 small onion, sliced
1 clove garlic, minced
1 tablespoon oil
1 8-ounce can tomato sauce
7-1/2 ounces can tomatoes, undrained and cut up
1 teaspoon Italian seasoning
3/4 teaspoon sugar
3 medium chicken breasts, skinless and boneless
1/2 cup ricotta cheese
3 tablespoons Parmesan cheese
1 tablespoon green onion, chopped
1/2 teaspoon Italian seasoning
Dash pepper
2 ounces mozzarella cheese, cut into thin strips

For sauce, in large saucepan cook celery, carrots, mushroom, onion and garlic in hot oil until onion is tender. Stir in tomato sauce, tomatoes, 1 teaspoon Italian seasoning and sugar. Bring to boiling, reduce heat. Cook, uncovered, over low heat for 20 minutes. Meanwhile, pound chicken breasts between 2 pieces of plastic wrap to 1/4 inch thickness. Combine ricotta cheese, Parmesan cheese, green onion, 1/2 teaspoon Italian seasoning and dash pepper. Place about 1-1/2 tablespoons of the cheese mixture on each chicken piece. Roll up; place seam side down in a 8x8x2" baking dish. Pour sauce over chicken rolls. Bake, covered, in a 375° oven for 25 to 30 minutes or until tender. Place mozzarella strips in a lattice design on top; bake 3 to 5 minutes more.
Makes 6 servings.

Southern Fried Chicken

3 quarts water
1 tablespoon salt
One 2 to 2-1/2 pound broiler-fryer chicken, cut up
1 teaspoon salt
1 teaspoon pepper
1 cup all purpose flour
2 cups vegetable oil
1/4 cup bacon drippings

Combine water and 1 tablespoon salt in a large bowl; add chicken pieces. Cover and refrigerate 8 hours. Drain chicken; rinse with cold water and pat dry. Combine 1 teaspoon salt and 1 teaspoon pepper; sprinkle half of mixture over all sides of chicken. Combine remaining mixture and flour in a gallon-size, heavy duty, zip top plastic bag. Place 2 pieces of chicken in bag; seal. Shake to coat completely. Remove chicken, and repeat procedure with remaining pieces. Combine vegetable oil and bacon drippings in a 12 inch cast-iron skillet or chicken fryer; heat to 360°. Add chicken, a few pieces at a time, skin side down. Cover and cook 6 minutes; uncover and cook 9 minutes. Turn chicken pieces; cover and cook 6 minutes. Uncover and cook 5 to 9 minutes more, turning pieces during the last 3 minutes for even browning. Drain chicken on a paper towel-lined plate placed over a large bowl of hot water. 4 servings. Serve with Fried Chicken Gravy.

Gladis, who works for the Tullars, makes the best fried chicken, claims Patti. Gladis soaks her chicken in the salted water before she coats the chicken with seasoned flour. She dips it in an egg beaten with a little milk. Finally she fries it in a cast iron skillet.

Fried Chicken Gravy

1/4 cup drippings from fried chicken recipe
1/4 cup all purpose flour
2 cups warm* milk or water
1/2 teaspoon salt
1/4 teaspoon pepper

Place drippings back in skillet. Over medium heat, add flour, stirring constantly until browned. Add milk or water gradually; cook, stirring constantly until thickened and bubbly (about 3 to 5 minutes). Stir in salt and pepper. Serve immediately. Yields 1-2/3 cups.

*Warming the milk or water helps to prevent lumping.

Chip, Michael Lee Grimes and his mother, Shirley in
North Carolina, 1996.

Chicken Curry

1 tablespoon butter
1 cup firmly chopped apple
1 cup sliced celery
1/2 cup chopped onion
1 clove garlic, minced
3 tablespoons cornstarch
2 to 3 teaspoons curry powder
3/4 cup cold chicken broth
2 cups milk
2 cups diced chicken
1 3-ounce can sliced mushrooms

In saucepan, melt butter; add apple, celery, onion and garlic.
Cook until onion is tender. Combine cornstarch, curry, 3/4 teaspoon salt and broth. Stir into onion mixture; add milk. Cook
and stir until mixture thickens and bubbles. Stir in chicken
and mushrooms. Heat through. Serve over hot, cooked rice and
pass condiments such as raisins, shredded coconut, chopped
peanuts and chutney; or serve in middle of East Indian
Rice Ring. Makes 5 or 6 servings.

East Indian Rice Ring

1/4 cup butter
1/2 cup chopped onion
1/4 cup slivered almonds
1/4 cup light raisins
6 cups hot cooked rice
Shredded coconut

In skillet, melt 1/4 cup butter; add onion and almonds. Cook until golden. Add raisins; heat until plump. Add rice and mix gently. Press mixture lightly into greased 6-1/2 cup ring mold. Unmold at once on platter. Fill with Chicken Curry and top with shredded coconut.

Italian Chicken

4 8-ounce boneless chicken breasts
1/2 pound margarine, melted
1 cup Italian dressing

Baste chicken breasts in melted margarine. Pour Italian dressing over chicken and bake for 20 minutes (or less) at 325°. Turn oven up to 375° and bake for 5 minutes more, until chicken turns golden brown. Chicken may be served cold the next day in a salad with dressing poured over it.

Note: Always pound chicken breasts with mallet to break down muscle tissue and to flatten. This not only tenderizes but reduces cooking time and shrinkage. This is an excellent dish to microwave and requires about 4 minutes cooking time.

Chicken with Spanish Sauce

3 pounds chicken pieces
1/4 cup flour
1 teaspoon salt
1/2 cup Spanish olive oil
2 garlic cloves, minced
1 small onion, minced
1/8 teaspoon cinnamon
1/8 teaspoon cloves
2 cups Rhine white wine
1/2 teaspoon salt

Coat chicken pieces in flour blended with salt. Fry in olive oil in skillet until very brown and crisp. Remove chicken; pour off all but 2 tablespoons oil. Add garlic, onion, cinnamon and cloves. Cook over moderate heat until onion is tender. Add white wine, simmer 10 minutes. Add salt if needed. Return chicken to skillet, cover and simmer gently about 20 minutes or until chicken is very tender. Makes 4 servings.

Oven-Fried Chicken

1 quart water
1 teaspoon salt
6 chicken drumsticks
4 bone-in chicken breast halves, skinned
1/2 cup nonfat buttermilk
3 cups cornflake crumbs
2 to 3 teaspoons Creole seasoning
2 teaspoons dried Italian seasoning
1/2 teaspoon garlic powder
1/8 teaspoon freshly ground black pepper
1/8 teaspoon ground red pepper
Vegetable cooking spray

Combine water and salt in a large bowl; add chicken pieces.
Cover and refrigerate 8 hours or overnight. Drain chicken;
rinse with cold water and pat dry. Place chicken in a shallow
dish; pour buttermilk over chicken, turning pieces to coat.
Combine cornflake crumbs and next 4 ingredients in a gallon-
size, heavy duty, zip-top plastic bag. Add red pepper. Place 1
piece of chicken in bag; seal. Shake to coat completely. Remove
chicken, and repeat procedure with remaining pieces. Place
coated chicken, bone side down, in a 15x10x1" jellyroll pan
coated with cooking spray, and spray chicken with
cooking spray. Place pan on the lowest rack in oven.
Bake at 400° for 45 minutes. Do not turn.
Yield: 6 to 8 servings.

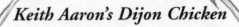

Keith Aaron's Dijon Chicken

4 chicken breasts, boneless and skinless
Salt and pepper to taste
Garlic powder to taste
1/2 cup sour cream
1/2 cup Dijon mustard
1/3 cup Italian-style fine breadcrumbs

Lightly sprinkle chicken with salt, pepper and garlic powder.
Combine the sour cream and mustard in a shallow dish, mixing
well. Dip each chicken breast in mixture and dredge in bread-
crumbs. Arrange in a single layer in baking pan. Bake at 325°
for 30 minutes or until done. Garnish with parsley, if desired.

Baked White Fish

8 ounce portion of white fish
(snapper, catfish, swordfish, flounder)
1/4 cup water
Juice of 1/2 lemon
Salt and Pepper
Lemon pinwheels

Lay fish portions on baking dish and pour water over fish.
Squeeze lemon juice over fish. Sprinkle with salt and pepper
and any other seasonings to suit your own taste buds.
Slice lemon pinwheels and place on each portion of fish.
Cover with aluminum wrap and place in oven.
Bake in 350° oven until fish is flaky.

Catfish Filet in
Butter Seasoning

1-1/2 pounds margarine
1 pound butter
1/8 teaspoon curry
1/2 teaspoon mustard powder
1/2 teaspoon rosemary
1 teaspoon garlic salt
1/2 tablespoon onion salt
1/2 tablespoon seafood seasoning
1/2 tablespoon Lawry's seasoning salt
1-1/2 tablespoons lemon juice

Mix all ingredients together and cook, do not boil, for 15 minutes over low heat.

When using for catfish, flounder or any other white fish, grill fish for 3 to 5 minutes on each side until fish is two-thirds cooked. Remove fish from grill and place into skillet with a portion of the mixed butter seasoning sauce. Cook for 5 more minutes over low heat, until done. Sauce may be thickened with cornstarch and water, if needed.

Fish may be prepared in the microwave and sauce applied near the end of cooking time.

Fish Potpourri

2 pounds fish fillets
(cod, sea bass or red snapper)
1/2 cup prepared pancake mix
2 tablespoons salad oil
2 medium sized onions, sliced
2 green peppers, seeded and cut in rings
2 stalks celery, thinly sliced
3 tomatoes, peeled and cut in quarters
1 clove garlic, minced
1 teaspoon salt
Dash pepper
3 8-ounce cans tomato sauce
2 tablespoons lime juice
1/8 teaspoon liquid hot pepper seasoning

Shake fish a few fillets at a time in a bag with the pancake mix;
shake off excess. Heat 2 tablespoons oil in a Dutch oven over
medium heat; put in as many fillets at a time as fit without
crowding and sauté until browned on both sides. Set aside; add
oil as needed to brown remaining fillets. When all fish is brown,
return to pan and arrange onion, green pepper, celery, tomatoes
and garlic over the top. Sprinkle with salt and pepper,
and pour over tomato sauce, lime juice and hot pepper
seasoning. Cover and simmer over very low heat
20 to 30 minutes or until fish flakes easily.
Makes about 8 servings.

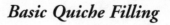

Basic Quiche Filling

1 pie shell
4 eggs
13-ounce can evaporated milk
2/3 cup milk
Salt and pepper to taste

Bake pie shell for 10 minutes. Cool slightly. Mix eggs and milk well. Layer desired ingredients in pie shell and pour mixture over top. Sample ingredients: crabmeat, shrimp, green onions, ham, Swiss cheese, green peppers, shrimp, mushrooms, onions. Bake at 325° until filling is set, approximately 30 to 45 minutes.

Enchiladas

1 dozen corn tortillas
1-1/2 pounds grated Monterey Jack cheese
8 ounces green chilies, diced
1 pint sour cream
Salt and pepper to taste
Oil for frying
1 or 2 7-ounce cans green chili salsa

Combine cheese, chilies, sour cream, salt and pepper. Heat oil and fry each tortilla for a few seconds. Keep limp; drain. Spread about 2 tablespoons cheese mixture on each tortilla and roll up. Reserve half the mixture. Place in a lightly greased shallow pan in a single layer. Spread remaining cheese mixture over top. Bake 25 minutes at 325°. Pass salsa separately. Serve with refried beans, tossed salad and heated, buttered flour tortillas.

Ronnie's
Beef Noodle Casserole

1 large bag of egg noodles
2 pounds hamburger meat
2 cans Cheddar cheese soup
3 to 4 cans tomato soup
1/2 cup diced onions
1/2 cup chopped bell pepper
Salt and pepper to taste
Garlic salt or powder to taste

Cook noodles according to package directions; drain. In a large saucepan brown hamburger and onions, drain off oil. Add noodles and onions; mix well. Add soups and remaining ingredients. Cook on low for about 20 minutes. You may want to add a little more tomato soup. This can be served nicely with garlic bread and salad.

Michael Lee, myself and Bill.

Ronnie's Noodle Casserole

1 large bag noodles
2 cans tuna, chicken or turkey, drained
1/2 cup celery, chopped
1/2 cup onion, chopped
1/2 cup bell pepper, chopped
3 to 4 tablespoons butter
3 to 4 tablespoons flour
2-1/2 cups milk
Salt and black pepper

Saute celery, onion, bell pepper in butter. Stir in flour, milk and meat. Mix well and add cooked noodles and seasonings to taste. May use 3 cans of cream of mushroom soup instead of making your own cream sauce. Serves 4-6 people.

Kimberly holding her son, Dohnte, Keith, Wilfred and Ronnie.

Cakes

- & -

Frostings

In addition to the recipes in this section
you'll find the following—

Bowl Cake

I sometimes had the creative grace to be able to transform mistakes into masterpieces. After buying a brand new pair of jeans, I inadvertently spilled some bleach down the side of one pant leg, stripping a patch of the fabric of color and ruining the jeans. Not one to throw away a brand new pair of pants, I whipped out a box of fabric paints and drew an ivy leaf freehand over the spot. I then painted an entire strand of ivy leaves running down the pant leg, and painted them a beautiful green edged in gold. I liked the effect so much I painted a strand of ivy leaves down the other pant leg, and in so doing created a chic, contemporary fashion statement out of what would have been a calamity.

So it is with food. Some of my best-loved desserts started out as barefaced disasters in my kitchen. The famous bowl cake is a case in point. Wanting to prepare an especially luscious and rich dessert for my family, I made a chocolate cake and doctored it up by slicing the cake layers into fourths and filling each layer with raspberries and whipped cream. In my enthusiasm to make the cake especially beautiful, I piled too much topping on the cake, and unable to support the weight, the cake broke in half and fell all over the place where I was working. I was horrified to find my beautiful cake ruined, and determined not to waste the delicious ingredients, salvaged my hard work by cutting the cake into pieces and placing it in a large bowl. I then artfully arranged more fresh fruit and whipped cream on top of what could have been a tragic misfortune. My family loved it, and when I was asked what it was called, I christened the concoction "bowl cake." It's been a family favorite ever since, and was very popular at Sunday brunches and when the family entertains. Here is the chocolate and raspberry variation of the cake; I also suggest using white cake with lemon filling accented with citrus fruit.

Bowl Cake

1 baked cake
Fresh fruit or pie filling
Whipping cream

Break cake into pieces and place in a pretty bowl. Alternate layers with fruit, toppings and whipped cream. Chill and serve.

Chip with President Clinton and Phil Leder, Director of SBA. The family won the State of Kentucky Small Business Person of the Year Award, 1995. The President is autographing our brochure. Chip had three goals: one, meet a president; two, be featured in Southern Living Magazine; and three, be on the Oprah show- 2 down, 1 to go.

Fresh Apple Cake

1-1/4 cups vegetable oil
2 cups sugar
3 cups flour
2 cups chopped apples
1 cup nuts
1 cup coconut
1 teaspoon salt
1 teaspoon baking soda
2 teaspoons vanilla
3 eggs

Combine oil and sugar; add dry ingredients alternately with eggs, beating after each addition. Add vanilla, chopped apple, nuts and coconut. Put in greased angel food pan. Bake for 1 hour, 15 minutes at 350°.

Topping:

1 cup sugar
1/4 cup milk
1 stick butter

A neighborhood friend of Patti's makes this special recipe, which she has enjoyed for many years.

142

Carrot Cake

2 cups sugar
3 cups all purpose flour
1 teaspoon soda
1/2 teaspoon salt
1 teaspoon cinnamon
2 cups carrots, grated
1-1/3 cups vegetable oil
2 eggs
1 cup nuts
1 cup drained pineapple
1 teaspoon vanilla extract
1 teaspoon lemon juice
1/2 teaspoon almond extract

In large bowl of mixer, mix together the sugar, flour, soda, salt and cinnamon. Add carrots, oil and eggs; beat at medium speed until well blended. Stir in remaining ingredients. Pour into two 10 inch cake pans and bake at 325° for 30 minutes.

*Y*ou can't change one item in a recipe without changing the others. One time, years ago, there were a couple of women in the restaurant kitchen, one of whom was Martha, and they didn't know how to bake anything. This was over 14 years ago, and now Martha is in charge of our baking department.

But anyway, the two women were baking pies one day and were complaining because they were having to stir so

Sour Cream Chocolate Cake

1/2 cup shortening
1-1/2 cups sugar
1/2 teaspoon vanilla
2 eggs
3 ounces unsweetened chocolate, melted and cooled
1/2 cup sour cream
1-3/4 cups all purpose flour
1 teaspoon soda
1/2 teaspoon salt
1 cup water

In large bowl of mixer, beat shortening and sugar until creamy. Add   vanilla and beat well. Beat in eggs, one at a time. Stir in chocolate and sour cream. Mix dry ingredients together in small bowl. Alternately add with water to cake mixture. Mix well. Pour into two 9" greased and floured baking pans and bake at 325° for 30-35 minutes.

much and for such a long time. They decided to put in an extra box of cornstarch, to help remedy the problem. What a mess. It turned out like cement! They didn't know that you couldn't just dump extra things in and have pudding.

If you are baking or cooking, you must use a recipe. I told them the only thing they could make, down at the restaurant without a recipe was stew. Ha Ha!

Nobby Apple Cake

3 tablespoons butter or margarine
1 cup sugar
1 egg
1 teaspoon baking soda
1 cup flour
1/2 teaspoon salt
1/4 teaspoon nutmeg
1/2 teaspoon cinnamon
2 cups diced apples

Blend all ingredients, except apples, with mixer. Fold in apples.
Bake at 350° about 30-35 minutes in a 9" square or loaf pan.

Miss Patti's Three Day Coconut Cake

1 Package Yellow Butter Cake Mix (2 layer)
6 or 7 ounces angel coconut
1 pint sour cream
2 cups sugar
1 large Cool Whip

Mix cake mix according to package instructions for two 8" cake
pans. Cool. Mix together coconut, sour cream, sugar and Cool
Whip. Split layers, making 4 layers. Spread mixture between
layers and all over outside. Sprinkle extra coconut all over outside. Place in refrigerator in air tight container for 3
days before serving. This is one of Patti's recipes the
restaurant uses and is just as popular as it ever
was. The only trick is keeping it on "hold"
for 3 days before serving.

Pumpkin Pound Cake

1 cup butter or margarine, softened
3 cups sugar
5 large eggs
3 cups all purpose flour
2 teaspoons baking powder
1/2 teaspoon baking soda
1/2 teaspoon salt
2 teaspoons ground cinnamon
1/4 teaspoon ground cloves
1/8 teaspoon apple pie spice
2 cups canned or cooked, mashed pumpkin
1/3 cup rum

Beat butter at medium speed with an electric mixer about 2 minutes or until soft and creamy. Gradually add sugar, beating at medium speed 5 to 7 minutes. Add eggs, one at a time, beating just until yellow disappears. Combine flour and next 6 ingredients. Combine pumpkin and rum. Add flour mixture to creamed mixture alternately with pumpkin mixture, beginning and ending with flour mixture. Mix at lowest speed just until blended after each addition. Pour batter into a greased and floured 10 inch tube pan. Bake at 325° for 1 hour and 25 minutes or until a wooden pick inserted in center of cake comes out clean. Cool cake in pan on a wire rack 10 minutes; then remove from pan and let cool.

Carrot Cake
From Patti's On The Pier

2 cups flour
2 cups sugar
2 teaspoons cinnamon
1 teaspoon salt
2 teaspoons baking soda
4 eggs
4 cups grated carrots
1 cup oil
3/4 cup chopped nuts

Combine flour, sugar, cinnamon, salt and baking soda in a bowl and set aside. In large bowl beat eggs until foamy. Slowly add oil. Add flour mixture a little at a time. Fold in carrots and nuts. Pour into two 8" greased and floured baking pans. Bake at 350° for 25 minutes.

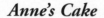

Anne's Cake

1 box chocolate cake mix
2 eggs, beaten
1 stick margarine or butter
1 cup pecans, chopped
6-ounce package chocolate chips
8-ounce package cream cheese
3 eggs beaten
1-pound box confectioners sugar
1/2 cup pecans

Combine dry cake mix, 2 eggs and margarine or butter. Mix well and spread in 9x13" pan. Sprinkle with 1 cup pecans and chocolate chips. Combine cream cheese, 3 eggs, confectioners sugar and 1/2 cup pecans; spread on top. Bake at 350° for 45 to 60 minutes.

Anne Ireland, Silver Cliff Inn

Chocolate Sour Cream Frosting

1 cup semisweet chocolate chips
1/4 cup margarine
1/2 cup sour cream
2-1/2 cups confectioners sugar

Microwave chocolate and margarine together in large microwaveable bowl until melted. Stir in sour cream and confectioners sugar.

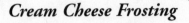

Cream Cheese Frosting

8-ounce package cream cheese
1 stick margarine
1 teaspoon vanilla
1 pound confectioners sugar

With mixer at medium speed, beat ingredients together until smooth and creamy.

Patti's Fluffy Frosting

1 cup milk
2 to 3 tablespoons flour
1/2 cup margarine
1/2 cup shortening
1 cup sugar

Cook milk and flour together until thick. Cool. Cream margarine, shortening and sugar together until smooth. Add milk mixture and beat until fluffy.

"This is the best frosting recipe in the world. I love it!"
Patti proclaims.

Candy, Cookies - & - Desserts

In addition to the recipes in this section
you'll find the following—

Patti's Candy

1 pound butter
1 18-ounce jar peanut butter
2 pounds powdered sugar (more if needed)
1 12-ounce package chocolate bits
1/4 cake grated paraffin

Cream first three ingredients together and roll into balls. Melt chocolate bits and paraffin together. Dip candy into chocolate mixture and place on greased pan or waxed paper and let set.

Mints

1 pound powdered sugar
4 tablespoons butter
4 tablespoons light cream
1/4 teaspoon oil of peppermint
Food coloring

Mix well and squeeze through pastry bag into flowerettes on to freezer paper. Freeze until used at which time they may be refrigerated.

Chocolate Nut Crisps

2 6-ounce packages butterscotch chips
1 6-ounce package semi-sweet chocolate chips
1 8-ounce can salted cashew nuts, chopped
1 16-ounce can Chinese noodles

Melt and blend chips in double boiler. Add nuts. Add noodles and blend until chopped fine. Drop by small spoonful on wax paper and cool.

Michael Lee's Spiced Shortbread Cookies

1 cup butter or margarine, softened
2/3 cup sifted confectioners sugar
1/2 teaspoon ground nutmeg
1/2 teaspoon ground cinnamon
1/2 teaspoon ground ginger
2 cups all-purpose flour

Cream butter; gradually add sugar, beating at medium speed of an electric mixer until light and fluffy. Add spices and beat well. Stir in flour. Shape dough into 1-1/4 inch balls, and place 2 inches apart on lightly greased cookie sheets. Lightly press cookies with a floured cookie stamp or fork to flatten to 1/4 inch thickness. Bake at 325° for 15-18 minutes or until done. Cool on wire racks.
Makes 2-1/2 dozen.

Orange Drop Cookies

1-1/2 cups packed brown sugar
1 cup butter or margarine
2 eggs
1 tablespoon grated orange peel
1 teaspoon vanilla
3 cups sifted all purpose flour
2 teaspoons baking powder
1 teaspoon baking soda
1/2 teaspoon salt
2/3 cup buttermilk

Cream brown sugar and butter or margarine; add eggs, orange peel and vanilla. Beat until fluffy. Sift together flour, baking powder, soda and salt. Add to creamed mixture alternately with the buttermilk, beating after each addition. Drop onto ungreased cookie sheet. Bake in 350° oven for 10 to 12 minutes. While cookies are warm frost with Orange Icing. Makes 6 dozen cookies.

Orange Icing:

1 tablespoon grated orange peel
3 tablespoons orange juice
3 tablespoons butter
3 cups sifted powdered sugar

Combine orange peel, orange juice and butter.
Stir in powdered sugar.

Potato Chip Cookies

1 cup butter or margarine
1/2 cup granulated sugar
1-1/2 cups sifted all purpose flour
1/2 teaspoon vanilla
1/2 cup potato chips, which have been pulverized in blender
1 cup finely chopped pecans or walnuts
Powdered sugar

In mixing bowl, cream butter or margarine with sugar. Blend in flour and potato chips. Stir in vanilla and pecans or walnuts. Drop by spoonful on ungreased cookie sheet and bake in 325° oven for about 12 minutes or until brown. Wait a couple of minutes before removing from pan. When almost cool, sprinkle with powdered sugar.

Congressman Ed Whitfield with Chip and Mike in Washington, D.C., 1995.

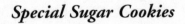

Special Sugar Cookies

1 cup powdered sugar
1 cup granulated sugar
1 cup butter
1 cup oil
2 eggs
1 teaspoon vanilla extract
1 teaspoon salt
1 teaspoon baking soda
1 teaspoon cream of tartar
4 cups plus 4 heaping tablespoons flour

Cream sugars, butter, oil, eggs and vanilla. Add dry ingredients; mix well. Roll into small balls. Flatten with bottom of a small juice glass that has been rubbed lightly with oil and dipped in sugar. Bake at 350° for 10 minutes. Makes approximately 100 cookies.

Snoozing on the freezer...

We only had two people working at Hamburger Patti's at the beginning so when we weren't busy I napped on top of the chest freezer. I worked so hard and was so tired that I had to get a quick snooze when I could do so and that was the best place I could find. It was the coldest!

Vanilla Chocolate Squares

1-1/4 cups sifted flour
1 teaspoon plus 3/4 cup sugar
1 teaspoon baking powder
1/2 cup, plus 6 tablespoons butter
1 egg yolk
5 teaspoons water
4 teaspoons vanilla extract
2 6-ounce packages chocolate chips
2 eggs
1-1/2 cups coarsely chopped walnuts

Grease a 9x13" baking pan. On wax paper sift together the flour, 1 teaspoon sugar and the baking powder; set aside. In a medium mixing bowl cream 1/2 cup butter with egg yolk, water and 1 teaspoon of the vanilla. Add flour mixture; blend well. Press mixture with fingers into bottom of prepared pan. Bake in a preheated 350° oven for 10 minutes. Remove from oven and sprinkle with chocolate. Return to oven until chocolate melts—about 10 minutes. Lightly spread chocolate with a small metal spatula; set aside. Meanwhile in a small mixing bowl beat eggs and 3/4 cup sugar until combined. Melt remaining 6 tablespoons butter; stir into egg-sugar mixture along with remaining 3 teaspoons vanilla and the nuts. Pour over chocolate layer in baking pan. Return to oven until browned, approximately 25 to 30 minutes. Cool on wire rack. If chocolate does not set, refrigerate until it hardens, about 15 minutes. Cut into squares.

Chocolate Brownies

8 squares unsweetened chocolate
3 sticks margarine
4 cups sugar
6 eggs
3 teaspoons vanilla
2 cups all purpose flour

Melt chocolate and margarine in double boiler. In large mixer bowl, combine sugar and chocolate mixture; blend well. Add eggs one at a time, mixing well after each addition. Mix in vanilla. Add flour and mix only until well blended. Pour into a 10x18 greased and floured baking pan. Bake in a 325° oven for 20 to 25 minutes. Don't overcook. These are supposed to be gooey! Cool and ice if desired.

Icing:

2 6-ounce packages of semi-sweet chocolate chips
1 cup milk
1 package powdered sugar
1 cup pecans

In microwave-safe bowl melt chips in for 2-1/2 minutes on high. Add milk and stir well. Slowly add powdered sugar until smooth. Spread over brownies and sprinkle with pecans.

Ginger Snaps

3/4 cup shortening
1/4 cup sugar
4 tablespoons molasses
1 egg
2 cups all purpose flour
2 teaspoons baking soda
1 teaspoon cinnamon
1 teaspoon cloves
1 teaspoon ginger
1 teaspoon nutmeg
Sugar

Combine shortening, sugar, molasses and egg until fluffy. Sift together flour, baking soda, cinnamon, cloves, ginger and nutmeg. Stir into molasses mixture. Form into small balls and roll in sugar. Place 2 inches apart on greased cookie sheet. Bake in 350° oven for 12 minutes.

Chocolate Crinkle Cookies

4 cups sugar
1-1/2 cups vegetable oil
1-1/2 cups Hershey's cocoa
8 eggs
4 teaspoons vanilla
4-2/3 cups all purpose flour
4 teaspoons baking powder
1 teaspoon salt
1 12-ounce bag of chocolate chips
Confectioner's sugar

In large bowl with electric mixer, beat sugar, oil, cocoa, eggs and vanilla. By hand stir in flour, baking powder, salt and chocolate chips. Refrigerate overnight. Roll into balls and place on greased cookie sheets. Bake for 18 minutes at 300°. Cool slightly on wire rack; roll in confectioner's sugar.

Old-Fashioned Shortbread Cookie

1 cup butter, softened
3/4 cup sifted confectioners sugar
1/4 cup cornstarch
1-3/4 cups all-purpose flour

Cream butter; gradually add confectioners sugar and corn-
starch, beating at medium speed of an electric mixer until light
and fluffy. Stir in flour. Chill several hours. Divide dough in
half. On greased baking sheet pat each half into 7" circle.
With fork pierce deeply to make 16 pie-shaped wedges. Bake at
300° about 30 minutes. Cool slightly; remove from pan.

Madonna's
Mountain Cookies

1 cup butter
1 cup confectioners' sugar
2 teaspoons vanilla extract
2 cups all purpose flour
1/2 teaspoon salt

Filling:
1 3-ounce package cream cheese, softened
1 cup confectioners' sugar
2 teaspoons all purpose flour
1 teaspoon vanilla extract
1/2 cup finely chopped pecans
1/2 cup flaked coconut

Topping:
1/2 cup semi-sweet chocolate chips
2 tablespoons butter
2 tablespoons water
1/2 cup confectioners' sugar

In a mixing bowl, cream butter, sugar and vanilla. Combine flour and salt; gradually add to the creamed mixture and mix well. Shape into 1 inch balls and place 2 inches apart on an ungreased cookie sheet. Make a deep indentation in the center of each cookie. Bake at 350 degrees for 10-12 minutes, or until the edges start to turn brown. Remove to wire racks to cool completely.

For the filling: Beat cream cheese, sugar, flour and vanilla in a mixing bowl, then add pecans and coconut. Mix well then spoon 1/2 teaspoon into each cookie.

For the topping:
Heat chocolate chips, butter
and water in a small saucepan
until melted. Stir in sugar and drizzle
over cookies. Makes 4 dozen.

Michael Lee's Orange Madeleines

1 cup butter, softened
3/4 cup sifted confectioners sugar
1 teaspoon grated orange rind
1 teaspoon orange extract
1-3/4 cups all purpose flour
Vegetable cooking spray

Cream butter; gradually add sugar. Beat at medium speed of
an electric mixer until light and fluffy. Add orange rind and
extract. Stir in flour. Press about 1-1/2 tablespoons dough
into madeleine molds lightly sprayed with cooking spray. Bake
at 325° for 20 minutes or until done. Invert onto wire racks
to cool. Makes 2-1/2 dozen.

Peanut Butter Cornflake Cookies

2 cups light corn syrup
1/2 cup brown sugar
2 cups creamy peanut butter
3 cups corn flakes cereal

Cook syrup and brown sugar in large pan until mixture begins
to boil. Reduce heat and stir in peanut butter. Add the
corn flakes until coated. Pour into a 9x13 buttered
pan and let cool. Slice into squares.

Michael Lee's
Praline Shortbread Cookies

1 cup butter, softened
3/4 cup firmly packed dark brown sugar
1-1/2 cups all purpose flour
1/2 cup ground pecans

Cream butter; gradually add brown sugar, beating at medium speed until light and fluffy. Stir in dough and ground pecans. Dough will be stiff. Divide dough into 6 equal portions; pat each portion to a 6 inch circle on lightly greased cookie sheets. Score dough into 8 wedges, using a fluted pastry wheel. Press outside edges of dough with tines of a fork. Bake at 325° for 20 minutes or until cookies are lightly browned. Let cool on cookie sheets; break into wedges. Makes 4 dozen.

Michael Lee and Chip with Newt - they were in Washington D.C. lobbying for National Restaurant Association, 1995.

Almendrado

2 envelopes gelatin
1 cup cold water
9 egg whites
1-3/4 cups sugar
1 teaspoon almond flavoring

Empty gelatin into cold water. Set cup in boiling water until gelatin melts. Beat egg whites until they stand in peaks. Continue beating and slowly add gelatin mixture, sugar and flavoring. Divide in 3 equal parts. Tint one part green. Coat a 9x13" pan with mayonnaise. Pour in the green Almendrado. Tint next part pink and smooth over first layer. Leave third layer white. Chill. Cut in squares and serve with sauce.

Almendrado Sauce

9 egg yolks
1 can condensed milk
1 can water
3/4 cups sugar
1-1/2 cups blanched almonds

Place all ingredients, except almonds, in a double boiler and cook until mixture thickens. When ready to serve, add chopped almonds and spoon over Almendrado.

This is from a friend in Tucson who went to
Jr. High School with me.

Michael Lee's
Mini-Mincemeat Nut Cakes

1/2 cup butter or margarine, softened
1/3 cup firmly packed dark brown sugar
3 eggs
2-1/2 cups all purpose flour
1 teaspoon baking powder
1/2 teaspoon baking soda
1 teaspoon salt
1 14-ounce can sweetened condensed milk
1 28-ounce jar commercial mincemeat
2 cups chopped walnuts

Cream butter; gradually add sugar, beating well at medium
speed of an electric mixer. Add eggs, one at a time, beating
after each addition. Combine flour, baking powder, soda and
salt; add to creamed mixture alternately with condensed milk,
beginning and ending with flour mixture. Mix just until
blended after each addition. Stir in mincemeat and walnuts.
Spoon batter into paper-lined miniature muffin pans, filling
3/4 full. Bake at 350° for 20 minutes or until wooden pick
comes out clean. Remove from pans, and cool
completely on wire racks.

Bread Pudding

3 tablespoons butter, melted
8 slices bread, torn in pieces
4 cups milk
1-1/2 cups sugar
4 eggs, beaten
1/3 cup raisins
1 teaspoon vanilla
1/2 teaspoon nutmeg or cinnamon

Combine butter, bread and milk. Stir in remaining ingredients, mixing well. Bake in a buttered 9x13" dish. Bake in 325° oven for 45 to 60 minutes or until brown and firm. Serve with Bourbon Sauce.

Bourbon Sauce

1 stick butter
1 cup sugar
1/4 cup water
1 egg, beaten
1/3 cup bourbon

In heavy saucepan, melt butter. Add remaining ingredients, stirring constantly until sugar dissolves. Serve on side.

Patti's
Pineapple Delight

1-1/2 large cans chunk pineapple
3/4 cup sugar
6 slices stale white bread, cubed
3/4 stick butter, softened

Drain pineapple. Mix juice and sugar. In large bowl mix bread and pineapple and add to sugar mixture. Pour into 9 x 12 baking dish. Spread butter over top. Bake in 300-325° oven for 1-1/2 to 2 hours until brown. Can also be served as a side dish.

Chip's Easy Chocolate Fudge Delight

1 box fudge brownie cake mix
Praline pecan ice cream
1 jar of fudge sauce, warmed
1 package chocolate after-dinner mints
1 jar marshmallow cream
Whipping cream, whipped
Maraschino cherries

Bake fudge brownie cake according to directions and cool. Slice cake and place individual serving on plate, then top with ice cream. Next top with fudge sauce which has been warmed together with the after-dinner mints. Then top with marshmallow cream, whipped cream and a cherry. Voila! Your guests will gasp.

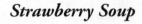

Strawberry Soup

4 cups frozen strawberries
1 cup Chablis wine
2 cups Sprite
Orange slices, mint sprigs and whipped cream for garnish

*Mix strawberries, wine and Sprite until strawberries just thaw.
Serve chilled after refrigerating for several hours with orange
slice on side of cup and mint sprig and dab of whipped cream
on top.*

Michael Lee's Coffee "N" Spice Pecans

1 tablespoon instant coffee granules
1/2 cup sugar
1/2 teaspoon ground cinnamon
Dash of salt
1/4 cup water
3 cups pecan halves, toasted

*Combine first 5 ingredients in a medium saucepan, stirring
until sugar dissolves. Add pecans, and bring to a boil. Cook 3
minutes, stirring constantly. Spoon onto wax paper, separating
pecans with a fork. Store in an airtight container.*
Makes 3 cups.

Patti's Pies

*P*atti and Bill never knew when the publicity would pay off. Just like when they got a letter from *Bon Appetit* asking for a recipe for "Sawdust Pie." Normally Patti did not give out recipes but she decided as long as it was *Bon Appetit* she would make an exception. Seems a lady from St. Louis had written to them and asked them to see if they could get this particular recipe. That mention was their first national publicity and they thank that lady and all of their customers for their help in bringing in all the national and regional attention. They have relied on word of mouth, "it's the very best, thanks everyone."

Patti's Sawdust Pie

7 egg whites, unbeaten
1-1/2 cups granulated sugar
1-1/2 cups graham cracker crumbs
1-1/2 cups pecans
1-1/2 cups coconut, flaked
9-inch unbaked pie shell
Sliced bananas
Whipped Cream

Mix first 5 ingredients together and stir by hand. Pour into unbaked pie shell. Bake in preheated 325° oven until glossy and set (about 25 to 30 minutes). DO NOT OVERBAKE! Center should be gooey. Serve warm with sliced bananas and whipped cream. Serves 8.

John Y. Brown Pie

1 cup sugar
1/2 cup all-purpose flour
1/2 cup melted butter
2 eggs, slightly beaten
6 ounce package butterscotch chips
1 cup chopped pecans
1 teaspoon vanilla
9-inch unbaked pie shell

Mix together sugar and flour. Add melted butter and blend well. Stir in eggs, chips, nuts and vanilla. Pour mixture into pie shell. Bake in a preheated 325° oven for one hour or until golden brown. Pie will wiggle when done; it sets as it cools. Serves 8.

Brown Sugar Pie

3 eggs
2 cups brown sugar, packed
4 tablespoons margarine, melted
9" unbaked pie shell

Preheat oven to 350°. In medium bowl, beat eggs and brown sugar together until smooth. Mix in margarine. Pour mixture into pie crust. Place on cookie sheet and bake for 45 minutes or until knife inserted in center comes out clean.

Patti's Kentucky Chocolate Pecan Pie

1 cup sugar
1/2 cup all purpose flour
1/2 cup melted butter
2 eggs, slightly beaten
6-ounce package chocolate chips
1 cup chopped pecans
1 teaspoon vanilla
1 unbaked 9 inch pie shell

Mix sugar and flour. Add butter, blend well. Stir in eggs, chocolate chips, pecans and vanilla. Pour mixture into pie shell. Bake in preheated 325° oven 1 hour, or until golden brown.

Note: This is a very rich pie. It is great right after it is baked, with ice cream or whipped cream. It can be refrigerated several days. Simply sprinkle water on top and microwave 10 seconds and it will be just like out of the oven.

Upside-Down
Strawberry Meringue Pie

3 egg whites
1/2 teaspoon vinegar
1/4 teaspoon salt
1/2 cup sugar
1/2 teaspoon vanilla
9" baked pie shell
3 cups fresh strawberries, divided
1/3 cup sugar
2 tablespoons cornstarch
1/2 cup water
Red food coloring
1 cup whipping cream

Beat egg whites with vinegar and salt to soft peaks. Gradually add 1/2 cup sugar and vanilla, beating to stiff peaks. Spread on bottom and sides of baked pie shell. Bake at 325° for 12 minutes, cool. Mash two cups strawberries. In saucepan, blend remaining sugar and cornstarch. Add water and berries. Cook until thick and boils. Cook two more minutes. Tint with food coloring. Cool slightly. Spread over meringue. Chill. Use whipping cream and whole berries for garnish.

"I always made this for my bridge club in California.
They also loved my pecan pie."

Patti's Cheesecake Pie

3-3/4 cups graham cracker crumbs
3/4 cup sugar
3/4 cup margarine, melted
5 8-ounce packages cream cheese, softened
1-3/4 cups sugar
3 tablespoons all purpose flour
1-1/2 teaspoons grated lemon rind
1-1/2 teaspoons grated orange rind
1 teaspoon vanilla extract
5 eggs
2 egg yolks
1/4 cup whipping cream
Fresh strawberries (optional)

Combine graham cracker crumbs, 3/4 cup sugar and margarine; stir well. Press mixture into two 10 inch pie plates. Beat cream cheese until soft and creamy. Gradually add 1-3/4 cups sugar, beating until fluffy. Add flour, citrus rind, and vanilla; mix well. Add eggs and yolks, one at a time, beating well after each addition. Stir in whipping cream. Pour filling into crusts and bake at 400° for 5 minutes. Reduce heat to 250° and bake an additional 30 minutes or until set. Chill for 8 hours or overnight. May be covered with plastic wrap and frozen. When ready to serve, top with strawberries and dollops of whipped cream. Makes two 10 inch pies or 29 small tarts.

Peanut Butter Pie

3/4 cup peanut butter
1-1/2 cups confectioners sugar
4-1/2 ounces cream cheese
1 12-ounce Cool Whip

Mix peanut butter, powdered sugar and cream cheese by hand until well blended. Fold in Cool Whip and pour in graham cracker crust. Refrigerate for two hours.

Graham Cracker Crust:

2 cups graham cracker crumbs
1/3 cup sugar
1/3 cup melted margarine

Mix ingredients and pat in 10 inch pie pan. Bake at 375°
for 8 to 10 minutes. Cool before filling.

When you think of Patti's, you think of desserts.

My father always loved desserts. Even if it was just a banana, I put cinnamon and sugar on it; then I poured cream on it. Dad would ask what we were having for dessert, so he would know how much to eat for dinner. He liked desserts the best.

So, it is no wonder that my specialties are "desserts." Like my mile-high meringue pies. I made 'em tall because you wanted everyone to stop and look at it. The pie was a real conversation piece, an attention getter.

At first I had problems with the meringue. My pies would weep. I was baking them twice a day so they would hold. Then one day a customer from nearby Dawson Springs told me that instead of cream of tartar, she would use a pinch of baking powder. The lady gave me a recipe for lemon meringue pie and I tried it and it worked. I baked and baked, varying my recipes each time and within 6 months I had the perfect formula. I had never before used baking powder but that was indeed the secret to my success.

I now share this success with my recipe for Coconut Pie with Mile-High Meringue.

From time to time I have cooking problems like anyone. Especially the Boatsinker Pie. "She makes chess pie the best," said her friend and chef, Curtis Grace, when he walked through my kitchen one day. I have never forgotten that. I was thrilled that he thought my recipe for chess pie was better than his!

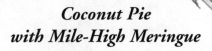

Coconut Pie
with Mile-High Meringue

Basic pudding filling:
3/4 cup sugar
3 tablespoons cornstarch
1/4 teaspoon salt
3 egg yolks, slightly beaten
2 cups milk
2 tablespoons butter
1 teaspoon vanilla

Combine dry ingredients and mix well. Add egg yolks and stir. Add milk. Cook slowly until thick, stirring constantly. After pudding is thick, add butter and vanilla. Pour into cooled, baked pie crust.

For coconut pie, add about 1 cup coconut.

For pineapple pie, add about 1 cup of well-drained crushed pineapple.

For chocolate pie, add 2 squares unsweetened melted chocolate or cocoa mixed with a little water that has been made into paste. Patti says the chocolate mixture must be fairly thick to prevent the filling from becoming too runny.

Meringue: Beat 4 egg whites with 1/2 teaspoon baking powder until stiff. Add 1/2 cup sugar and blend well. Cover pie with mixture. Make sure to seal the filling to edge of crust or pie will weep. Brown in oven approximately 15 minutes.

Craig and Ashleigh of Ashleigh's boutique. Craig is a Senior
Master Chief in naval reserves and works for the Naval
Engineer Department as an underwater diver today.

1995. Craig, Ashleigh and Cindy. Craig and Cindy met at
our Christmas Eve Church Service and he married the
Kentucky girl, Miss Cindy Bonnell.

Custard Pie

3 egg yolks
4 eggs
1/2 cup sugar
1/4 teaspoon salt
1/2 teaspoon vanilla
3 cups warm milk
1 unbaked pie shell
Nutmeg

Beat egg yolks and eggs by hand until fluffy. Add sugar, salt, vanilla and milk and pour into pie shell. Bake in 325° oven for 50-60 minutes or until knife comes out clean. Sprinkle nutmeg on top.

Pecan Pie

4 eggs
1 egg yolk
1 cup sugar
1/2 cup melted margarine
1-1/2 cups dark corn syrup
1-1/2 cups pecans
1 unbaked pie shell

Beat eggs, egg yolk and sugar until combined. Stir in margarine, corn syrup and pecans. Pour into pie shell. Bake for 1 hour at 350°.

"This is a wonderful recipe which I've used for years. Bill says 'it's a lady's pie' but I think both men and women love it."

Patti's On The Pier

Several years back our family decided to open a new restaurant on Green Turtle Bay. It was a beautiful setting for a restaurant, and we called it Patti's on the Pier. Michael managed Patti's on the Pier, and it was here that he met his future wife, Lawana, who was hired as a hostess, while working part time and going to college.

I remember the brunches were beautiful, with customers lined up to eat. I went to work at 1:00 a.m. to prepare for the Sunday brunch, making the cheese grits and the sausage gravy for the biscuits and all the desserts. I worked

Double Crust Raisin Pie

1-1/2 cups brown sugar
4 tablespoons corn starch
3 cups raisins
3/4 teaspoons orange peel
3/4 cups orange juice
3/4 teaspoons lemon peel
3/4 tablespoons lemon juice
1-3/4 cups cold water
Pastry for double crust pie, unbaked

Combine ingredients and cook in double boiler until thick. Pastry line the pie dish. Pour raisin mixture into crust and top with second crust. Pierce crust with fork. Bake 45-60 minutes in 325° oven.

by myself all night long and had a wonderful time—no interruptions.

As a special treat for the staff, when I finished preparing for the customers I would make strawberry donuts for the crew and customers who came in when we opened the restaurant at 10:30 a.m. I always had the fresh, hot donuts waiting for them. If there were any left over, I would take them to the piers at Green Turtle Bay and give them away, which served to draw a lot of hungry boaters into the restaurant! See page 84 for recipe. Patti's on the Pier was open for about four years, and it is a fond memory for the Tullar family and all those who enjoyed the good food and company that were found there.

Pumpkin Pie

3/4 cups brown sugar
1/2 teaspoon salt
1 teaspoon cinnamon
1/2 teaspoon ginger
1/4 teaspoon ground cloves
1/2 teaspoon nutmeg
1-1/2 cups pumpkin
2 eggs, beaten
1 can evaporated milk
1 tablespoon molasses
1 unbaked pie shell

Combine brown sugar, salt and spices. Add remaining ingredients and mix until smooth. Pour into pie shell. Bake 350° for 15 minutes then turn down to 325° for 10 more minutes.

Michael T. loves to do pretty things. He was in charge of the beautiful brunch at the Pier. He gets frustrated in the restaurant kitchen because there is no time to do 'pretty' things. Everything moves at such a fast pace. Preparing a beef roast in the oven is not much fun or exciting. At Bill's you had the dessert buffet so you could bake all kinds of delicious pies and cakes and keep them in the refrigerator.

Cream Cheese Pineapple Pie

Pineapple Layer:
1/3 cup sugar
1 tablespoon cornstarch
8-ounce can crushed pineapple, undrained

Cream Cheese Layer:
8-ounce package cream cheese,
softened to room temperature
1/2 cup sugar
1 teaspoon salt
2 eggs
1/2 cup milk
1/2 teaspoon vanilla
1/4 cup chopped pecans

9" unbaked pie shell

Combine sugar, cornstarch and pineapple in a small saucepan. Cook over medium heat, stirring constantly until mixture is thick and clear. Cool; set aside. Blend cream cheese, sugar and salt in mixer bowl. Add eggs, one at a time, beating after each addition. Blend in milk and vanilla. (If mixture looks slightly curdled, don't worry—it bakes out.) Spread cooled pineapple layer over bottom of pie shell. Pour cream cheese mixture over pineapple; sprinkle with pecans. Bake at 400° for 10 minutes; reduce heat to 325° and bake for 50 minutes. Cool.

Chocolate Chip
Pecan Pie

1 cup sugar
1/2 cup all purpose flour
1/2 cup melted butter
2 eggs, slightly beaten
6 ounce package chocolate chips
1 cup chopped pecans
1 teaspoon vanilla
9-inch unbaked pie shell

Mix together sugar and flour. Add melted butter and blend well. Stir in eggs, chips, nuts and vanilla. Pour mixture into pie shell. Bake in a preheated 325° oven for one hour or until golden brown. Pie will wiggle when done; it sets as it cools. Serves 8.

French Silk Pie

1 pound butter
3 cups sugar
8 tablespoons cocoa
1 tablespoon vanilla
8 eggs
1 baked pie shell

Cream butter and sugar until creamy. Add cocoa, vanilla and eggs one at a time, mixing well after each addition. Spoon into a cooled baked pie shell. Refrigerate until firm 3 to 4 hours. Garnish with shaved chocolate. Refrigerate any leftovers. Time consuming, but well worth it! Beat eggs one at a time.

Turtle Pie

3 cups chocolate ice cream
2-1/2 cups chocolate chip mint ice cream
3 cups vanilla ice cream
2 cups hot fudge
2 cups caramel
1 graham cracker crust

Layer ice creams, hot fudge (cold) and caramel into the graham cracker crust. Freeze until ready to serve.

Chess Pie

2 cups sugar
1 stick butter
6 egg yolks
1 tablespoon corn meal
1 tablespoon flour
1 teaspoon vanilla
1 13-ounce can evaporated milk

Cream together sugar and butter. Add yolks, mixing well. Fold in remaining ingredients. Pour into unbaked pie shell and bake at 350° until set, approximately 30 minutes.

Sour Cream-Lemon Pie

1 cup sugar
3-1/2 tablespoons cornstarch
1 tablespoon lemon rind, grated
1/2 cup fresh lemon juice
3 egg yolks, slightly beaten
1 cup milk
1/4 cup butter
1 cup cultured sour cream
1 baked 9 inch pie shell
1 cup heavy whipping cream, whipped
Lemon twists for garnish

Combine sugar, cornstarch, lemon rind, juice, egg yolks and
milk in heavy saucepan; cook over medium heat until thick.
Stir in butter and cool mixture to room temperature. Stir in
sour cream and pour filling into pie shell. Cover with
whipped cream and garnish with lemon twists.
Store in refrigerator.

I received a recipe from a friend
for a pie that was supposed to be absolutely extraordinary. The
only problem was the recipe did not give precise measure-
ments, only approximations — approximately this and
approximately that. The other problem was that my pan was
bigger than the pie pan called for in the recipe, so I decided to
double the recipe and make two pies, using the high end of
each approximate measurement, figuring that since I was
making two pies I would go all out. I put the pies to bake in
the restaurant's big, old-fashioned cast iron oven. Soon melted caramel, chocolate and coconut were flowing all over the

Boo Boo Pie

2-2/3 cup coconut
1 can sweetened condensed milk
1 stick margarine
3 squares unsweetened chocolate
3/4 cup sugar
1/2 cup all purpose flour
3 eggs
1 tablespoon vanilla

Mix together coconut and sweetened condensed milk; set aside.
Microwave margarine and chocolate together for 4 minutes in a
microwave bowl. Add remaining ingredients and pour into a
greased pie pan. Put coconut mix around top. Bake in a
325° oven for 25 minutes.

oven like lava from Mt. Vesuvius. The sweet, sticky mess coated the inside of the oven from front all the way to the back. I
had to crawl inside the oven to clean it out, and the oven was
so huge it swallowed me up completely, leaving nothing but
my feet hanging out. Someone came by and asked what I was
doing, and I said it was the worst boo boo I had ever made
and the pie's name stuck. I brought what was left of the pies
home and fed them to my children, and they loved them. I
redid the pie a few days later - baked exactly the way it was
supposed to be— but the children liked the "Boo Boo" pie
better. I now have figured out a way to keep the pie in the pie
pan and it isn't such a boo boo anymore. Try this recipe for
one of the best-selling pies, and see if you agree.

Boatsinker Pie

5 sticks butter
1 cup dark corn syrup
7-1/2 ounces unsweetened chocolate
3 cups sugar
9 eggs
3 teaspoons vanilla
2 unbaked pie shells

Microwave butter and corn syrup in microwave bowl for 9 minutes on high.   Stir well. Add unsweetened chocolate and microwave an additional 4 minutes. Place sugar in a large bowl; stir in eggs and vanilla by hand until well mixed. Stir in the chocolate mixture. Pour evenly into the 2 unbaked pie shells and bake at 325° for 22 minutes and reduce heat to 275° for an additional 25 minutes. Cool before serving. Add any type ice creams and topings to fit your taste buds.

Chocolate Chess Pie

2-1/4 cups sugar
6 heaping tablespoons cocoa
Pinch of salt
3 eggs, beaten
3/4 stick margarine, melted
1 12-ounce can evaporated milk
1-1/2 teaspoons vanilla
1 unbaked pie crust

In large bowl, combine sugar, cocoa and salt. Add remaining ingredients and pour into unbaked pie crust. Bake 30-40 minutes in 325° oven.

Wonderful chocolate pie—
best I ever had because it is so smooth.

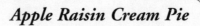

Apple Raisin Cream Pie

Pastry for 2 crust, 10 inch pie
7 to 8 cups tart apple slices, 1/8 inch thick
1 cup sugar
1/2 cup flour
1/2 teaspoon nutmeg
1 teaspoon cinnamon
3/4 cup raisins
Dash salt
1 to 2 teaspoons grated lemon rind
1 tablespoon (rounded) butter
3/4 cup heavy cream

Make favorite pastry; line bottom of pie plate with one crust and set aside. Combine apple slices, sugar, flour, spices, raisins, salt and lemon peel; mix together well. Spoon filling into pastry-lined pan; dot with butter. Cover with top crust decorated with steam vents; seal edges. Cut a one inch circle from dough in center of top crust. Bake at 400° for 40-45 minutes. Remove pie from oven; slowly pour cream into center hole of top crust. Return to oven; bake 5-10 minutes longer. Let stand 5 minutes before cutting. Refrigerate leftovers.

Shaker Lemon Pie

2 large lemons
2 cups sugar
5 eggs well beaten
1 unbaked pie shell

Slice lemons paper thin with a serrated knife; remove seeds. Add sugar and let stand 5 hours or overnight. Blend eggs into lemon mixture. Turn into unbaked shell. Bake 350° until set.

Once our kids grew up I needed 4 more to feel like my nest was fun again. The loves of my life, Callie, Elkie, Sassy and Doll.

Sweet Potato Pie

2-1/2 cups sugar
1 teaspoon cinnamon
1 teaspoon nutmeg
4 eggs
2 cans evaporated milk
2 teaspoons vanilla
4 cups mashed sweet potatoes
2 unbaked pie shells

Topping:

2/3 cups margarine
2/3 cup flour
1 cup brown sugar
1 cup coconut
1 cup pecans

Mix all the dry ingredients. Beat the eggs; add milk and vanilla. Blend into the dry ingredients; fold in sweet potatoes. Pour into the two unbaked pie shells. Bake at 400° for 15 minutes; reduce heat to 325° for 15 minutes. In the meantime, combine topping ingredients. Sprinkle over pies and bake an additional 10-15 minutes until golden brown.

Creme de Menthe Pie

2 8-ounce packages cream cheese
1-1/2 cups confectioners sugar
4 tablespoons creme de menthe
2 cups whipping cream, whipped

Crust:
2 cups crushed chocolate cookies
1/4 cup melted margarine

In mixer, beat cream cheese, powdered sugar and creme de men-the until creamy. Fold in whipped cream. Pour into crust. Chill and garnish with shaved chocolate or fresh mint.

My littlest angels, Anna & Arielle, 1997.

Transparent Pie

2 tablespoons butter or margarine
1 cup sugar
3 egg yolks, beaten
5 tablespoons cream
1 teaspoon vanilla
1 unbaked pie shell

Cream butter and sugar. Add egg yolks and cream; mix well. Add vanilla and pour into pie crust. Bake 30 minutes at 375°. Top with meringue and brown at 350° for about 15 minutes.

Meringue:
3 egg whites
6 tablespoons sugar

Beat egg whites until stiff. Gradually beat in sugar.

The Lemon Angel Pie recipe (at right) is from Mary Jane Reece, a friend for over 50 years from California, who was in my bridge club.

Cookie Crust

1/2 cup butter or margarine
2 tablespoons sugar
1 cup flour

Cream butter and sugar together. Add flour and mix until well combined. Bake at 375° for 12 - 15 minutes.

Lemon Angel Pie

Crust:
4 egg whites
1/4 teaspoon cream of tartar
1 cup sugar

Beat egg whites and cream of tartar until stiff but still moist. Gradually add sugar and beat until glossy. Pour in well greased pie dish and shape as a crust. Bake at 300° for 1-1/2 hours.

Filling:
4 egg yolks
1/2 cup sugar
Juice and rind of 1 lemon
1/2 pint whipping cream, whipped

In double boiler, mix egg yolks, sugar, juice and rind of lemon until thick. Cool. Fold in half of the whipped cream and pour into pie shell.   Smooth rest of whipped cream over top. Refrigerate 24 hours before serving.

Walnut Pumpkin Pie

1 graham cracker pie crust
1 15-ounce can pumpkin
1 14-ounce can sweetened condensed milk
1 egg
1-1/4 teaspoons ground cinnamon, divided
1/2 teaspoon ground ginger
1/2 teaspoon nutmeg
1/2 teaspoon salt
1/4 cup packed brown sugar
2 tablespoons all purpose flour
2 tablespoons cold margarine or butter
3/4 cup chopped walnuts

Heat oven to 425°. In mixing bowl, combine pumpkin, sweetened condensed milk, egg, 3/4 teaspoon cinnamon, ginger, nutmeg and salt; mix well. Turn into pie crust. Bake 15 minutes,
remove pie. Reduce oven temperature to 350°. In small bowl,
combine sugar, flour and remaining 1/2 teaspoon cinnamon;
cut in margarine until crumbly. Stir in walnuts. Sprinkle
walnut mixture evenly over pie. Bake 40 minutes or until knife
inserted 1 inch from edge comes out clean. Cool. Garnish as
desired. Refrigerate leftovers. Makes 8 servings.

Rhubarb Pie

7 cups rhubarb, cut in 1" pieces
2-1/2 cups sugar
5 eggs
5-1/2 tablespoons tapioca
3 tablespoons butter
Pastry for single crust pie plus lattice top crust

Place pastry in pie plate for bottom crust. Mix together rhubarb, sugar, eggs and tapioca. Place in pie crust. Slice and dab butter over top of rhubarb. Place lattice over top. Bake in 425° oven for 10 minutes; reduce to 350° and bake 45 additional minutes.

Try using a package of frozen strawberries along with a package of rhubarb for a nice variation.

Lawana's
Chocolate-Mint Cheesecake

Crust:
1 9-ounce package chocolate wafer cookies, broken
1/4 cup sugar
1/2 cup unsalted butter, melted and cooled

To make the crust, crush cookies and sugar together to form fine crumbs. Add the melted butter and process until the crumbs begin to stick together. With your hand draped with plastic wrap to form a glove, press the crumbs firmly onto the bottom and all the way up the sides of a 9 inch springform pan. Wrap aluminum foil around the outside of the pan. Position a rack in the middle of oven and preheat oven to 350°.

Filling:
10 ounces bittersweet chocolate, chopped
2 pounds cream cheese, at room temperature
1-1/4 cups sugar
1/3 cup unsweetened cocoa
1 teaspoon peppermint extract
4 large eggs, at room temperature

Melt the chocolate, stirring constantly, until smooth. Remove from heat; set aside. In a large bowl, combine the cream cheese and sugar. With an electric mixer, at medium speed, beat until smooth. Beat in the cocoa and peppermint extract. Add the

*eggs, one at
a time, beating after each
addition, until just combined. Add
the melted chocolate and beat until smooth,
stopping occasionally to scrape down the sides of
the bowl. Pour the filling into the crust (it will almost
completely fill it). Bake until the center is just set, about 50
minutes. Cool. Cover with aluminum foil and refrigerate
overnight or for up to 4 days. To serve, run a knife around the
pan sides to loosen the cake. Remove the foil from the pan and
release the pan sides. May garnish with mint leaves and pipe on
whipped cream. Top with chocolate shavings. Cut into wedges.
Serves 12 people.*

Ashleigh, Anna, Arielle - my angels.

Freezer Story

Early one morning I found myself alone in the restaurant two hours before anyone else was scheduled to arrive. I needed to get frozen items out of the big "walk-in" freezer so I could start preparing for the breakfast rush. I let myself in and started looking for what I needed when, to my horror, the heavy freezer door clicked shut behind me. The walk-in was an older model and ice had formed a tight seal around the door, effectively locking it shut and sealing me in tighter than a tomb. The safety latch that should have allowed me to open the door was also frozen solid and couldn't be budged.

Fighting back panic, I grabbed an industrial-size can of peaches and began to gently and rhythmically pound against the lock, knowing that if I hit the lock too hard it would snap off and it would be hours before anyone found me. Shivering with cold, I continued to gently pound the lock until finally, to my immense relief, the latch gave way and I was able to open the door and escape into the warmth of the kitchen. I later found out I had been in the freezer so long I was only about 15 minutes from severe hyperthermia. From that point on, I have had a special place in my heart for peaches. Being forever grateful to the can of peaches that saved my life and prevented me from turning into an ice cube, I give this peach-lover's recipe as a testament to my "great escape."

Dutch Peach Pie

2 eggs, beaten
2 tablespoons margarine, melted
1 can sweetened condensed milk
2 cups peaches
1/3 cup sugar
3/4 cup all purpose flour
6 tablespoons butter
1/2 cup chopped pecans
Pastry for single crust pie

Bake pie crust at 400° for a few minutes. Pour peaches into crust. Mix eggs, margarine and sweetened condensed milk together. Pour over peaches. In medium bowl mix sugar and flour; cut in butter until crumbly. Put streusel topping on pie and sprinkle with pecans. Bake at 350° for 20 minutes. Will be done when wooden pick inserted in middle comes out dry.

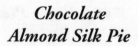

Chocolate Almond Silk Pie

Crust:
1 cup all purpose flour
1/3 cup finely chopped toasted almonds
6 tablespoons butter
3 tablespoons confectioners sugar
1/4 teaspoon vanilla

Filling:
3 cups sugar
1 pound butter
8 tablespoons cocoa
1 tablespoon almond extract, or almond flavored liqueur
8 eggs

Whipped cream
Sliced almonds

Combine all crust ingredients and blend with mixer on low speed until well mixed, 2-3 minutes. Press on bottom and sides of 9 inch pie pan; bake at 400° for 8-10 minutes. Cool. To make filling, combine sugar and butter in mixer bowl; beat at medium speed until light and fluffy. Add cocoa and almond extract or liqueur; beat until well mixed. Add eggs, one at a time, beating 2 minutes after each addition. Spoon filling into cooled crust; refrigerate until firm, 3 to 4 hours. Garnish with whipped cream and sliced almonds. Keep refrigerated.

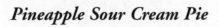

Pineapple Sour Cream Pie

3 egg whites, room temperature
1/2 cup sugar
2 tablespoons all purpose flour
1 20-ounce can crushed pineapple
8 ounces sour cream
3 egg yolks
1 baked 9" pie shell
1/2 teaspoon vanilla
1/4 teaspoon cream of tartar
6 tablespoons sugar

In saucepan combine sugar and flour; stir in undrained pineapple and sour cream. Cook over medium heat until thickened and bubbly. Reduce heat; cook and stir for 2 minutes more. In bowl, slightly beat egg yolks. Gradually stir in 1 cup of hot pineapple mixture; return all to saucepan. Bring to a gentle boil. Cook and stir for 2 more minutes. Pour hot filling into baked pie shell. For meringue, add vanilla and cream of tartar to egg whites in bowl. Beat with an electric mixer on medium speed about 1 minute or until soft peaks form. Gradually add the sugar, 1 tablespoon at a time, beating on high speed for about 4 minutes or until mixture forms stiff, glossy peaks and sugar is dissolved. Spread meringue onto hot filling making sure to completely cover pie. Bake in 350° oven for 15 minutes or until meringue is golden. When cool, refrigerate for 3 to 6 hours before serving. Very good, one of my favorites for the last 40 years.

Madonna's Caramel Delight Pie

1 cup pecans, chopped
1 7-ounce package flaked coconut
1 stick butter or margarine
1 8-ounce box cream cheese
1 can sweetened condensed milk
1 16-ounce container Cool Whip
1 jar caramel ice cream topping
2 graham cracker pie crusts

In a skillet, brown pecans and coconut in butter; set aside. Blend cream cheese and condensed milk together; add all of the Cool Whip. Divide into pie crusts. Top with the coconut-pecan mixture, then drizzle the caramel topping over the top. Keep refrigerated.

Pat Wood's Lemon Meringue Pie Custard

2 cans sweetened condensed milk
1-1/2 cups lemon juice
4 egg yolks
4 egg whites
6 tablespoons sugar
Baked pie shell

Mix sweetened condensed milk and egg yolks thoroughly. Add lemon juice and mix well. Pour into baked pie shell. Beat egg whites and sugar until whites are stiff. Spread meringue over custard. Bake at 350° for 12 to 15 minutes. Chill to set.

Patti's Side

& Miscellaneous

Dishes

In addition to the recipes in this section
you'll find the following—

Broccoli Quiche

1 unbaked pie shell
1 box frozen broccoli
4 eggs
1/2 teaspoon salt
3 tablespoons Parmesan cheese
1/3 cup grated Cheddar cheese

Prebake pie shell at 400° for 10 minutes. Defrost broccoli in steamer for 15 minutes. Turn oven down to 350°. Beat eggs slightly; add salt and 2 tablespoons Parmesan cheese. Add grated Cheddar cheese. Stir to combine. Chop broccoli and add to egg mixture. Pour into pie shell and sprinkle with remaining Parmesan cheese. Bake for 20-25 minutes. Slice into 10 slices.

Potatoes Au Gratin

1 clove garlic
Butter
1/4 pound grated Cheddar cheese
2 cups sliced, cooked and peeled potatoes
Salt and pepper to taste
2 eggs, beaten slightly
1 cup milk
1/2 teaspoon salt
1/4 teaspoon nutmeg
2 tablespoons butter

Rub a baking dish with garlic which has been split; butter dish.
Sprinkle half of the Cheddar cheese in the dish. Cover evenly
with potatoes.   Sprinkle with salt and pepper. Mix eggs, milk,
salt and nutmeg. Pour over the potatoes. Cover with
remaining cheese and dot with butter. Bake 45
minutes at 350°. Serves 4.

Copper Pennies

4 cups carrots or beets
1 onion, sliced
1 green pepper, sliced
1/4 cup sugar
2 tablespoons vinegar
3 tablespoons salad oil
1/4 cup tomato soup
1 teaspoon dry mustard
1 teaspoon Worcestershire sauce

Cook carrots or beets until crisp tender. Combine remaining ingredients and pour over vegetable. Let marinate in refrigerator for 24 hours. Serve cold.

We served this recipe in the buffet line at the Pier for Sunday brunch.

*O*ne night a group of young college boys were celebrating, having an especially good time. and asked their server if they could meet this woman named Patti. I had to laugh because I knew what to expect when I walked out. These young fellows were awaiting a young beauty, because of all the old photographs of me we have in the dining room, and here I came, an old lady. Their jaws dropped when I came out to their table. It's more fun to be like Betty Crocker, and never age. I don't want my picture to be taken as an old lady, it's more fun the other way.

Patti's Sweet Potato Casserole

9 cups sweet potatoes, drained
1-1/2 cups brown sugar
1/2 cup sugar
2 tablespoons vanilla
6 eggs
Salt to taste
1-1/2 sticks margarine, melted
1 can evaporated milk

Topping:
1-1/2 cups brown sugar
1 cup flour
3 cups pecans
1 stick margarine

Mash sweet potatoes and combine with remaining ingredients,
except topping.   Pour into greased pan. Bake at 325° for 30
minutes. Combine topping ingredients until crumbly.
Put topping on last 10 minutes of baking.

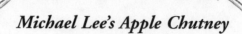

Michael Lee's Apple Chutney

8 cups peeled and chopped tart apples
4-1/2 cups sugar
2 cups seedless golden raisins
1 cup coarsely chopped toasted pecans or walnuts
1/2 cup vinegar
Peel of 2 oranges, finely chopped
1/3 teaspoon cloves

Combine all ingredients in large kettle or Dutch oven. Place over high heat and bring to rolling boil, stirring constantly. Reduce heat to simmer and cook slowly until apples are tender and syrup is very thick and almost caramelized. Ladle into hot sterilized jars, seal and store in cool, dark, dry place. Keep refrigerated after opening. May also be frozen. Very good served with chicken over rice.

1997, Chip and I are both wonderfully colorful people. We both love life dearly. Notice the cross I gave him for Christmas.

Country Club Squash

5 tender small squash
Salt and pepper to taste
1 tablespoon butter
3/4 teaspoon chicken base
1 tablespoon grated onion
1 egg, well beaten
1 cup sour cream
3/4 cup bread crumbs
3/4 cup sharp Cheddar cheese, grated
Paprika

Cut and cook squash until tender. Mash and add salt, pepper, butter, chicken base and onion. Add well beaten egg and sour cream. Pour into baking pan. Combine breadcrumbs, shredded cheese and paprika. Sprinkle over top of squash. Bake at 350° for 30 minutes. Serves 8 to 10.

Michael Lee's
Stewed Tomatoes and Okra

2 28-ounce cans whole tomatoes with juice
1 8-ounce package frozen okra, steamed
3 inside stalks of celery with leaves, thinly sliced
1/2 large bell pepper, diced
1 medium onion, diced
3 slices of white bread, broken into pieces
2-1/2 teaspoons dried oregano
2-1/2 teaspoons dried basil
2-1/2 teaspoons salt
1-1/2 teaspoons pepper
1 tablespoon garlic juice

Cut out tomato cores and quarter large tomatoes; halve small
tomatoes. Cook tomatoes and juices, celery, bell pepper, onion,
bread and spices for 30 minutes and simmer. Add okra
and cook an additional 30 minutes on very low
simmer. Adjust seasonings if necessary.

Michael Lee's
Spinach-Stuffed Squash

6 firm medium yellow squash
10 ounce package frozen chopped spinach
1/2 cup sour cream
1/2 tablespoon butter
Seasoned salt to taste
1/2 onion, chopped or onion salt
Black pepper to taste
Saltine cracker crumbs
Grated Parmesan cheese

Wash squash and cut in half lengthwise. Scoop out seeds and discard. Cook in salted water until barely tender. Drain. Cook spinach. Drain well. Combine spinach with sour cream, butter, salt, onion and pepper. Stuff squash with spinach mixture. Sprinkle with cracker crumbs and cheese. Bake at 325° for 30 minutes. Serves 6 to 12. Zucchini may be substituted for yellow squash.

Michael Lee's
Peach Chutney

4 pieces ginger root
1 tablespoon pickling spice
1-1/2 cups cider vinegar
2 cups sugar
1 29-ounce can peaches, drained and cut in pieces
1 cup seedless raisins
1 hard pear, peeled, sliced and chopped
12 pitted dates
1 hot red pepper, broken
1 teaspoon tumeric
1 clove garlic, minced
1/4 teaspoon salt
1/2 pound small onions, chopped

Pound the ginger root, combine it with the pickling spice, and tie loosely in a cheesecloth bag. Put it in a large kettle with the vinegar and sugar and bring it to a boil. Drain the peaches. Boil the peach liquid until there is only 1/2 cup remaining. Add the fruits, red pepper, tumeric, garlic and salt to the vine-gar mixture. Simmer, without a cover, for about 1-1/2 hours, stirring occasionally. Add the onions after the first hour of cooking. When it is thick, remove the spice bag.
Pour into jars and seal. Makes about 6 half pints.

Michael Lee's
Baked Cranberry Sauce

4 cups fresh cranberries
2 cups sugar
1/2 teaspoon ground cinnamon
1 13-ounce jar orange marmalade
3 tablespoons lemon juice
1 cup coarsely chopped walnuts, toasted

Wash and drain cranberries; place in a large bowl. Combine sugar and cinnamon; add to cranberries, mixing well. Spoon into a 9 inch square pan; cover with foil. Bake at 350° for 45 minutes. Add orange marmalade, lemon juice and walnuts, mixing well. Store in refrigerator. Makes 4 cups.

My loving daughter, Ronnie, with dad. She came to take care of me during my illness in 1996.

Strawberry Butter

3/4 pound margarine or butter
16 ounces frozen strawberries
1/2 cup powdered sugar

Bring margarine or butter to room temperature and whip. Let strawberries thaw. Whip all ingredients together, including strawberry juice, with large mixer. Fresh strawberries can be used in season. Vary amount of sugar to taste. (Increase when using frozen berries and decrease when using fresh berries).

Regular Butter

1/2 pound butter
1/4 pound margarine

Whip until fluffy.

Strawberry Butter

A long, long time ago a tiny restaurant in Corbin, Kentucky was begining to make a name for itself and its excellent fried chicken. Gil Cummings, who worked in Shoney's test kitchens and also with Colonel Sanders in the fried chicken restaurant, stopped by Patti's one day, and after tasting the delicious flower pot bread told Mr. Bill that I should try a recipe for strawberry butter that was similar to the one being tested by Colonel Sanders at the time. I tried it, and history was made. Now when customers come to Patti's they are served our famous flower pot bread with strawberry butter. The strawberry butter is available in the gift shop to take home and is delicious served on toast, muffins, or just about anything!

Whipped Lemon Butter

1/2 cup soft butter or margarine
1 tablespoon minced parsley
1 teaspoon chopped chives
1/2 teaspoon salt
Dash of cayenne pepper
3 tablespoons lemon juice

Cream butter until soft and fluffy. Add parsley, chives, salt and cayenne pepper. Mix well; add lemon juice, about 1/4 tablespoon at a time, stirring until well blended. Serve over hot asparagus, broccoli, cauliflower or spinach. Makes about 3/4 cup. To keep, place in jar, cover and store in refrigerator. Before serving, let stand at room temperature until slightly softened.

Patti's Cranberries

1 package fresh cranberries
2 cups sugar
1/2 cup dark rum

Mix ingredients in a large covered baking dish. Bake at 325° for one hour. Uncover and bake for an additional hour.

Sherried Walnuts

1 tablespoon butter softened
1-1/2 cups sugar
1/2 cup dry sherry
1/2 teaspoon cinnamon
1/8 teaspoon nutmeg
2 cups walnut halves

Butter baking sheet. Combine sugar and sherry in heavy saucepan and bring to a boil over high heat stirring until sugar dissolves. Cook briskly, undisturbed, to 240° on candy thermometer or until forms a soft ball in ice water. Remove from heat; add cinnamon, nutmeg and walnut halves. Stir gently until syrup becomes opaque and creamy. Spread on baking sheet and carefully separate walnuts with two forks. Cool at room temperature and store in airtight jar.

Strawberry Dips

1 quart fresh strawberries with stems
1 cup sour cream
Powdered sugar

Dip strawberries into sour cream; coat with powdered sugar to serve. 6 servings.

Freezer Pickles

2 quarts cucumber slices,
(remove peel if desired)
2 onions, sliced thin
2 teaspoons pickling salt
1-1/4 cups white vinegar
1-1/4 cups sugar

Combine cucumbers, onions and pickling salt. Let stand for 2 or more hours with ice cubes on top. Heat vinegar and sugar. Stir to dissolve sugar; let cool. Drain excess liquid from cucumber mixture. Pour sugar-vinegar mixture over cucumbers; mix well and pack into freezer containers. Freeze and allow to age at least 2 weeks before defrosting and using. Refrigerate after opening.

"Growing up in Arizona in the desert, we didn't have gardens. I never canned vegetables but I did freeze these pickles."

Salsa Fria

4 ripe tomatoes peeled, cored and chopped
1 large onion, chopped
1 medium green pepper, chopped
1 can green chilies
1 clove garlic, minced
1 tablespoon vinegar
1 tablespoon olive oil
1 teaspoon salt
1/4 teaspoon coriander

Mix and chill.

Weights and Measures

3 teaspoons=1 tablespoon

4 tablespoons=1/4 cup

5-1/3 tablespoons=1/3 cup

8 tablespoons=1/2 cup

10-2/3 tablespoons=2/3 cup

12 tablespoons=3/4 cup

16 tablespoons=1 cup

1 ounce=28.35 grams

1 gram=0.035 ounces

1 cup=8 fluid ounces

1 cup=1/2 pint

2 cups=1 pint

4 cups=1 quart

4 quarts=1 gallon

8 quarts=1 peck

4 pecks=1 bushel

1 quart=946.4 millimeters

1 liter=1.06 quarts

Emergency Substitutions

1 cup cake flour=1 cup minus 2 tablespoons all purpose flour   (in custards)

1 tablespoon cornstarch (for thickening)=2 tablespoons flour or 4 teaspoons quick-cooking tapioca

1 teaspoon baking powder=1/4 teaspoon baking soda plus 1/2 cup buttermilk or sour milk (to replace 1/2 cup of liquid called for in recipe)

1 cake compressed yeast=1 package or 2 teaspoons active dry yeast

1 cup whole milk=1/2 cup evaporated milk plus 1/2 cup water or 1 cup reconstituted nonfat dry milk plus 2-1/2 teaspoons butter or margarine

1 cup sour milk or buttermilk= 1 tablespoon lemon juice or vinegar plus sweet milk to make 1 cup (let stand for 5 minutes)

1 whole egg-2 egg yolks

1 square (1 ounce) unsweetened chocolate= 3 tablespoons cocoa (regular type, dry) plus 1 tablespoon butter or margarine

1 tablespoon fresh snipped herbs=1 teaspoon dried herbs

1 small fresh onion=1 tablespoon instant minced onion, rehyrdrated

1 teaspoon dry mustard=1 tablespoon prepared mustard

1 clove garlic=1/8 teaspoon garlic powder

1 cup tomato juice=1/2 tomato sauce plus 1/2 water

1 cup catsup or chili sauce=1 cup tomato sauce plus 1/2 cup sugar and 2 tablespoons vinegar (for use in cooked mixtures)

How Much and How Many

Butter, chocolate
2 tablespoons butter=1 ounce
1 stick or 1/4 pound butter=
 1/2 cup
1 square chocolate=1 ounce

Crumbs
28 saltine crackers=1 cup
 fine crumbs
14 square graham crackers=
 1 cup fine crumbs
22 vanilla wafers=1 cup fine
 crumbs
1-1/2 slices bread=1 cup soft
 crumbs
1 slice bread=1 cup fine dry
 crumbs

Cereals
4 ounces macaroni (1 to 1-1/4
 cups)=2-1/4 cups cooked
4 ounces noodles (1-1/2 to 2
 cups)=2 cups cooked
7 ounces spaghetti-4 cups
 cooked
1 cup packaged precooked rice=
 2 cups cooked

Fruits, vegetables
Juice of 1 lemon=3
 tablespoons
Grated peel of 1 lemon=
 1 teaspoon
Juice of 1 orange=about
 1/3 cup
Grated peel of 1 orange=
 about 2 teaspoons
1 medium apple, chopped=
 about 1 cup
1 medium onion, chopped=
 1/2 cup

Cream, cheese, eggs
1 cup whipping cream=
 2 cups whipped
1 pound American cheese,
 shredded=4 cups
1/4 pound blue cheese,
 crumbled=1 cup
12 to 14 egg yolks=1 cup
8 to 10 egg whites=1 cup

Nuts
1 pound walnuts in shell
 =1-1/2 to 1-3/4 cups
 shelled
1 pound almonds in shell=
 3/4 to 1 cup shelled

Index

*H*amburger Patti's Ice Cream Parlor grew from my mom's dream into reality in 1977.

Grand Rivers was a sleepy, economically depressed town, where a dog could wander aimlessly down Main Street without fear of ever being hit by a car. Today, this sleepy little town has risen like a "phoenix of old" into a bustling tourist metropolis. Through our customer base, life has been breathed back into many businesses and given our community back a personal sense of pride and hope for the future. We are seeing this through the completion of a new community senior citizen's building, new businesses moving into town, construction of sidewalks, upgrading of schools for our children and increased living standard for all.

Currently, Patti's is the second largest employer in the county. We employ up to 180 people, creating an annual payroll of $1,500,000.00.

Mom's cookbook is a prelude to future additions. We plan, in the Spring, to begin construction on a new animal park, children's playground and two new specialty stores. The stores will be the first, in many years, to be built on Main Street. As they become successful, more will be built and attract more retailers to our community.

As the company continues to grow, so do our personal dreams. Our plan for the very near future is to build a "pay for lake fishing" pond for the children, condominiums and a bed & breakfast for our guests to stay in, a chapel for weddings, receptions and other purposes. Michael Lee is always working to expand our commercial foods division. We are anxious for a reuniting of our family, working and living together in Grand Rivers, as Craig (now living in Washington, D.C.) gets close to retirement from the Navy and Ronnie (now living in California) has her children raised and living independently on their own.

In conclusion, let me say, in 1976 after getting out of the Navy and hitchhiking from Norfolk, Virginia to Grand Rivers to visit my family, I felt the Lord was leading me to build a little place on earth where people could come, even if for a few hours, to relax and forget their troubles. To the Lord and all His goodness, I give my thanks. I truly feel that He alone was instrumental and worked through me to build this very special place for all of you to share. Until our paths cross again, may God bless you folks and keep you in His arms.

William (Chip) D Tullar J.

The Tullar Family
Bill, Patti, Ronnie, Chip, Craig,
Michael Lee, Michael T., Lawana,
Arielle and Anna

Mail to: *Patti's 1880's Settlement*
Attn: Gift Shop
P. O. Box 111
Grand Rivers, KY 42045

For orders call: 502-362-8844
Discover, Visa & MasterCard accepted
Credit Card #_____ Exp. Date_____

Please send me _____ copies of **Miss Patti's Cookbook**

@ $17.95 each	_____
Postage and handling 3.50	_____
KY residents add 6% sales tax 1.08 each	_____

Patti's Specialty Items

Patti's Pork Chop Seasonings

6 oz. Shaker	$ 4.99	_____
12 oz. Jar	$ 7.49	_____
16 oz. Jar	$10.99	_____

Patti's Pork Chop Sauce

12 oz Jar	$ 7.49	_____
16 oz. Jar	$10.99	_____

Patti's Homemade Strawberry Butter

12 oz. Jar	$ 4.99	_____
Patti's Preserves, Jams and Jellies	$2.69 to $4.69	_____

Patti's Homemade Loaf Bread

2 lb. Loaf	$ 2.99	_____

Patti's Homemade Pies $ 7.99

Sawdust Pie, Boo Boo Pie	_____
Chocolate Chip Pecan Pie	_____
Butterscotch Chip Pecan Pie	_____

Total   _____

6% State sales tax and shipping will be added to each order.

(KY checks only) Make check payable to *Patti's 1880's Settlement*
Ship to:

_____

_____

_____